MW00685507

A Case Study Approach to
Ecology Field Studies
Third Edition

By John C. Jahoda, Kevin D. Curry, and Christopher P. Bloch
Bridgewater State University

Kendall Hunt
publishing company

Cover image © John C. Jahoda

All images provided by John C. Jahoda and Kevin D. Curry

Kendall Hunt
publishing company

www.kendallhunt.com
Send all inquiries to:
4050 Westmark Drive
Dubuque, IA 52004-1840

Copyright © 2009, 2011 by Kendall Hunt Publishing Company
Copyright © 2009 by Bent Tree Press

ISBN 978-0-7575-9475-5

All rights reserved. No part of this publication may be reproduced,
stored in a retrieval system, or transmitted, in any form or by any means,
electronic, mechanical, photocopying, recording, or otherwise,
without the prior written permission of the copyright owner.

Printed in the United States of America
10 9 8 7 6 5 4 3 2 1

Table of Contents

CHAPTER 1

Introduction

"Nature is full of genius, full of diversity: so that not a snowflake escapes its fashioning hand."

—Henry David Thoreau (from his "Journal")
American Writer and Philosopher (1817-1862)

This laboratory manual is designed to support a laboratory and field experience in a one-semester course in general ecology. The case study approach is taken to introduce the student to ecological field studies, the handling of data and the process of science. The entire scientific process is modeled in a series of case studies, including observation, formation of hypothesis, data collection, data analysis, and presentation of results in the format of a scientific research paper.

The overall goal in this course is to learn as much as possible about the principles of ecology. The focus is on systems ecology and the ecosystem as the basic unit of ecological structure and function. The course models science as a process of discovery. Students work as research teams in a series of ecological case studies designed to model scientific investigations and procedures.

THE MAJOR OBJECTIVES OF THE COURSE INCLUDE:

1. To lay the bare essentials of a groundwork for understanding the basic principles of ecology.
2. To look at the process of ecological change both in the long term (evolutionary change) and in the short term (succession).
3. To model the process of science through ecological field studies focused on local ecosystems.
4. To model the way in which scientists handle data. This will include all aspects of data gathering and analysis, including the use of statistical methods and computers for analysis of data sets.
5. To model the primary method by which scientists communicate with their peers: by writing original research papers.

Science is a process of discovery. A scientist's life is dedicated to the adventure of discovery. Thus, active collaboration is the way scientists do their job in the "real world" of scientific investigation. However, this joy of discovery is often missing in the typical college classroom. In this course, we will approach the subject as scientists do, with an emphasis on discovery. Scientists usually work as teams. Being a good team member is a key to being a good scientist. Thus, the learning experience in this class will model the team approach taken by practicing scientists.

In a series of four case studies, students will work in research teams to gather data. After the data are gathered, the students will work together to analyze the data collected. In two of the studies, research teams will exchange and share data with other research teams.

Each student will turn in one laboratory report in the form of a scientific paper in ecology. For the other three case studies each student will turn in a brief letter report. The format for the scientific paper and the letter reports are covered in Chapter 7.

A number of points are worth mentioning that will help the student understand the parameters of this course.

1. Your grade is <u>based on your demonstrated mastery of the subject and material</u>. It is not competitively based. There is no scale or limit to the number of good grades that can be achieved. If everyone demonstrates superior mastery of the subject, everyone can earn an "A."

2. Research Teams.
    The laboratory research team will be the team that you will work with in the laboratory. Laboratory research teams will be limited to two students per team and will be numbered with a combination of a number for the lab section and a letter designation (1A, 1B, 1C, 1D, etc.). Members of a research team will work together to gather data during the four case study field trips. To the extent possible both members of the research team should also be in the same lecture section and in the same lecture section base group.

3. Field Teams.
    In the field, two research teams will combine to form a four-person field team to gather data. Although working together with the other research team to gather the data, each research team should keep its own data sheet and record all field data.

    Data gathering will always be a collaborative activity carried out by a field team composed of two research teams working together. Data analysis and report writing will be carried out in the laboratory. The data belongs to everyone who participated in gathering the data in the field. Each student is responsible for turning in his or her own reports. You may work alone in the analysis or you may work together with other students. We recommend working together, because this approach will help you develop collaborative skills which will be important to you not only in this course, but also in other courses, and in the "real world" once you leave college and become involved in a career or a job. Preparing students to live in the real world includes making classroom experiences more similar to career situations, more reflective of the increased interdependence in the world, and more realistically aimed at building a high quality of life within and after college.

LABORATORY AND FIELD PROCEDURES

LAB REPORTS are due on the dates listed in the course syllabus.

Laboratory reports are of two kinds
   A.   Short letter reports for three of the case studies.
   B.   A major report in the form of a scientific paper for intertidal zonation case study.

The major report must follow accepted scientific format for laboratory research reports as outlined in chapter 4 of McMillan (2006). Additional information is provided in Chapter 7 of this lab manual.

MAKE-UP REQUIREMENTS FOR MISSED FIELD TRIPS

Students who miss any of the four field trips, for whatever reason, will not receive full credit for any laboratory report dealing with that field trip. Because the gathering of data is a key component of any research project, missing this phase of the case study represents a serious lack of participation in the process of science.

Therefore, students who miss the field trip must make up the field trip and turn in a supplemental make up report along with the scientific paper report or letter report for the case study in order to receive a grade for the case study report. Case study reports will not be graded unless the required make-up report is submitted along with it.

The supplementary report for the missed field trip should include the following:

   1.   Photographs of the site.
   2.   Photographs showing you at the site.
   3.   Photographs showing each of the four focal animals for the study (Intertidal Zonation Trip) or habitat types (Macroinvertebrate Trip) or habitat areas of the pond (Plankton Trip) or tree types (Tree Competition).
   4.   Data obtained following the directions given in the laboratory case study. For the Intertidal zonation case study you should run a transect according to the directions in the lab and make counts at all three tidal locations using the methodology as described in the lab handout. For the macroinvertebrate case study you should do a sweep and collect several macoinvertebrates. For the plankton diversity case study you should use a plankton net to sample the plankton, and for the Tree Diversity case study you should present data taken on one focal tree from each size category following the procedure in Chapter 8.

You may borrow field equipment that will be necessary for the study. These items can be checked out and then checked back in with your instructor, your lab instructor, or one of the departmental support staff.

REPORTING RESEARCH RESULTS

Each individual student will prepare a complete written report on the intertidal zonation field study. This report will follow the format of a standard scientific paper, such as would be published in a journal such as *Ecology*. Students should refer to the assigned style manual (McMillan 2006). In addition, examples of papers are easily obtained from journals in the library. Chapter 7 of this lab manual presents more details on how to properly write and format a scientific paper.

The grading rubric that will be used to evaluate the research report will be posted on the course web site. It is recommended that you review this rubric in order to understand how the report will be evaluated by your instructor. Once a report is submitted, the instructor will evaluate it and return it with suggestions for improvement. You will then have the option to revise and resubmit the paper to improve the grade.

For the other three case studies, each student will prepare and submit a short letter report discussing the result of the case study. This letter report must include complete information about the study, including location, procedures, results, discussion, and recommendations. An example of a letter report can be found in Chapter 7.

PROCEDURES

Procedures for the field studies will be discussed in laboratory and in the field. Teams are responsible for proper upkeep of all assigned space and equipment. Laboratory periods will be devoted to demonstration of techniques and procedures and work on field research case studies as listed on the course syllabus. In many cases, the actual measurements must be taken in the field. Whenever possible, samples should be collected in the field and transferred to the laboratory for analysis. Laboratory analysis is preferable to field analysis because there is more control over variables and working conditions are vastly superior to the field. Samples of the biota can be transferred to collecting buckets, glass jars, or plastic bags. Water samples must be transferred in clean water sample bottles. Care must be taken to use a bottle appropriate to the test. All samples collected in the field to be taken back to the laboratory for more analysis must be completely labeled with all relevant data including date, where the sample was collected, time the sample was collected, conditions of collection, as complete an identification of the sample as possible, and the name(s) of the collector(s). Data sheets for recording data will be provided. All data must be reported in metric units: mg/1, 0C, ppm, ppt, cm^2, m^2, etc.

> "When we try to pick out anything by itself, we find it hitched to everything else in the universe."
>
> —John Muir

LITERATURE CITED

McMillan, V. E. 2006. *Writing Papers in the Biological Sciences*. Fourth Edition Bedford/St. Martin's Press. New York.

C H A P T E R 2

Introduction to Statistics and Data Analysis

WHY DO WE USE STATISTICS: OR, HOW DO WE CHARACTERIZE THE FOREST WHEN WE CAN ONLY SEE SOME OF THE TREES?

The use of statistical analyses in ecological research is important because statistics allow us to draw conclusions about a *population* based on a *sample* of individuals from that population. A *population* is the complete set of all individuals of interest in a study. A *sample* is the subset of the population that is actually observed in the study. An example will illustrate this.

Suppose you were interested in the biology of the invasive Asian shore crab. Some invasive species grow larger in their new habitats than they do in their native range, possibly because of differences in environmental conditions or an absence of competitors in the new habitat (e.g., Leger and Rice 2003). If this is true of the Asian shore crab, you might expect that the average size of Asian shore crabs in the United States will be larger than that of those still living in Asia. How would you test this hypothesis?

If you wanted to be absolutely certain of the answer, you would need to measure the size of every Asian shore crab in the United States and every Asian shore crab in Asia, and calculate average body size for each group. That way, you would know the "true" average size of shore crabs from each continent, and it would be easy to compare the two numbers to determine whether they are the same. In reality, though, it would be impossible to measure each and every Asian shore crab on two continents. In fact, it is almost always impossible to observe an entire population. Instead of trying to do so, we observe a smaller number of individuals (a subset that we call a *sample*) from each population and assume that the characteristics of the sample are similar to the characteristics of the whole continental or regional population. If that assumption is true, then we can use our measurements from the sample to draw conclusions about the whole population.

THE PROBLEM OF SAMPLING ERROR AND CHARACTERIZING ENTIRE POPULATIONS

Using a statistic to draw conclusions about a population is complicated by *sampling error*. Sampling error is simply the difference between a particular characteristic for a sample (a *statistic*) and the same characteristic of the whole population (a *parameter*). The existence of sampling error doesn't necessarily mean that anything was done incorrectly; rather, it's a natural consequence of sampling. If we were to take a random sample of 25 Asian shore crabs and measure their shells, we can expect the average shell size from that sample to be similar to the average shell size for the whole population, but it is very unlikely to be exactly the same.

Moreover, no two samples will be identical. Because each sample from the same population will include different individuals, there always will be variability in the specific characteristic between samples. If we were to take a second sample of 25 Asian shore crabs, we would expect average shell size of this second sample again to be similar to that of the whole population, but it would probably not be exactly the same as the average shell size for the whole population or the previous sample. If we were to take an infinite number of samples, however, we can expect that *most* of them would have an average (or *mean*) shell size that would be close to the true mean for the entire population. Nevertheless, because of variability among individuals (i.e., because of sampling error), we would also expect a small number of samples to yield means that are far from the mean for the whole population (Figure 2-1).

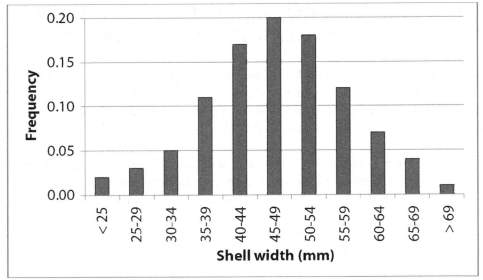

Fig. 2-1. A hypothetical frequency distribution for shell width of Asian shore crabs. In this hypothetical population, the population mean is 46.2 mm. Most samples drawn from this population have means near this value, whereas fewer than 5% of samples had means less than 25 mm or greater than 69 mm.

THE VALUE OF SAMPLE STATISTICS

The value of using statistics in scientific studies is they provide an objective way to test hypotheses. Most statistical hypothesis tests are conceptually rooted in the *rare event rule*: if, according to a given assumption (hypothesis), the probability of an event occurring is very small, but the event is observed anyway, we conclude that the assumption is probably false (Triola and Triola, 2006). To see how this works, consider the following example. Suppose that we want to compare mean shell size between Asian shore crabs from Massachusetts and those from Maine. Suppose further that the Massachusetts crabs come from the population depicted in Figure 2-1. If we believe that crabs from Maine experience similar environmental conditions and similar availability of food to those in Massachusetts, we might expect them to grow at similar rates. Therefore, our hypothesis might be that mean shell width is equal in the two populations. If this hypothesis is true—if shell width really is the same, on average, for crabs in Maine and Massachusetts—then we should expect that a sample drawn from the Maine population will have a similar mean shell width to that of the Massachusetts population. Suppose we sampled the Maine crabs and found that their mean shell size was 22.5 mm. What would this signify? Based on our knowledge of the Massachusetts population shown in

Figure 2-1, we know that it would be very unlikely for a sample to have such a small mean if it came from a population with a mean shell size as high as that in Massachusetts (46.2 mm). In fact, we would expect such a result from only 2% of samples! Our results are clearly not consistent with our hypothesis: if the two populations had equal mean shell sizes, we would not expect such a small mean shell size in the sample from Maine, even as a result of sampling error. Consequently, our best conclusion is to reject the hypothesis that the two populations have equal shell size, in favor of an alternative hypothesis that the crabs in Massachusetts are, on average, larger. We could then begin to search for biological explanations for this observed phenomenon. These further studies could involve additional analysis of our original data, or they might require more detailed field studies or experiments.

HOW WE USE STATISTICS

There are two major types of statistics: *descriptive statistics* and *test statistics*. As their names imply, descriptive statistics are used to describe the characteristics of the population from which a sample was taken, whereas test statistics are used to test particular hypotheses about populations. There are many different descriptive statistics and many types of test statistics. We will address some common ones below, and in additional detail in Chapter 9.

Descriptive Statistics

Descriptive statistics are numbers that we calculate based on the data we collect in a sample, with the assumption that the sample is representative of the population as a whole. If this is true, then we can consider the descriptive statistic to be a good estimate of what we would obtain if we censused the entire population. The mean (see Chapter 9) is a good example. If we calculate the mean shell size for a sample of Asian shore crabs, we are hoping that this tells us something about the mean shell size for the whole population from which we sampled.

The problem with an estimate of the mean (and this is true of most statistics) is that it is impossible to know how close it is to the "true" mean for the whole population. Because of sampling error, we know that estimates of the mean will differ between samples, even if those samples come from the same population. So, how different must two statistics be before we conclude that there is a "real" difference between them that cannot be explained simply by sampling error? In other words, how different must two statistics be before we conclude that the two samples probably came from different populations? This is why we need measures of variability.

Measures of Variability

One of the most common measures of variability is the *standard deviation* (see Chapter 9). This statistic measures how individual data points are distributed around a mean: the greater the standard deviation, the more dispersed or "spread out" the data are (Fig. 2-2). Although this information is useful in its own right, the standard deviation has another important property. It can be used to derive *confidence intervals* (sometimes abbreviated "CI"), which can then be used to test hypotheses about means.

Unlike a single point estimate of a parameter (e.g., the mean), a confidence interval provides a range of values that is likely to contain the "true," or *parametric*, value of the parameter (i.e., it is a range of plausible values for the parameter of interest). In ecology, as with most biological research, we most often use 95% CIs. In other words, we wish to derive a range of values such that we can be 95% confident that it will include the parametric value. (Recall that, because of sampling error, we can almost never be 100% confident of our estimates; 95% confidence is not bad, though. If you answer 95% of the questions correctly on your next ecology exam, you will probably be pretty happy.)

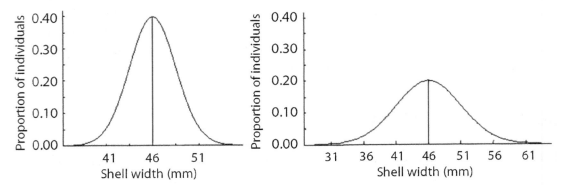

Fig. 2-2. Two hypothetical distributions of shell width in Asian shore crabs.
Note that in the distribution on the left, shell widths are much more tightly clustered around the mean than in the distribution on the right. Because the sample depicted on the right has much more variable measurements, it would have a larger standard deviation. This greater variability would also result in a larger 95% confidence interval—in more variable populations, it is more difficult to obtain a precise estimate of the mean.

Comparing means using 95% CIs

Suppose you want to compare two means. For example, you might want to compare average shell width of Asian shore crabs between populations in Maine and Massachusetts. Or you might want to compare average population density of shore crabs between rocky shores and sandy beaches, or between higher and lower elevations. The possibilities are limited only by the researcher's imagination. Here, we will discuss how to make such a comparison.

There are many statistical techniques that can be used to test for differences between means. Some of these methods are quite complex. We, however, will use a fairly simple approach: comparing means and confidence intervals. Once we collect our data, we will calculate a mean and 95% CI for each group we wish to compare (later, we will demonstrate how to use Microsoft Excel to do these calculations). We will then examine the confidence intervals to see whether they overlap. Recall that the 95% CI around a sample mean contains the range of most likely values of the parametric mean. If the 95% CIs of two means do not overlap (see Fig. 2-3), then the most plausible values for one mean are different from the most plausible values for the other. In such a case, the difference between means is greater than you would expect from sampling error alone. You can safely conclude that the difference between the two means is *significant*—in other words, that it probably was caused by something more than sampling error. In many cases, significant differences between means are caused by real biological differences between groups. Perhaps crabs in Massachusetts grow faster because the climate is warmer. Perhaps crabs are more abundant on rocky shores than on sandy beaches because they have greater access to shelter and food. The statistics can tell us whether there is a difference between the means, but as biologists, we must then seek the cause of those differences.

We've stated that we can conclude that a significant difference exists if the 95% CIs do not overlap. Conversely, we might expect that if CIs overlap at all, we should conclude that there is no significant difference (i.e., that the degree of difference we see is small enough to be caused by sampling error alone). This usually works. There are some situations, though, in which 95% CIs can overlap slightly, but a more sophisticated statistical test would find a significant difference (Julious, 2004). As such, you should be aware that our approach to comparing means is conservative—we will occasionally fail to find a difference that really exists. However, if the CIs overlap greatly—especially if the mean of one group falls within the CI of the other group—then you can be confident in concluding that there is no significant difference.

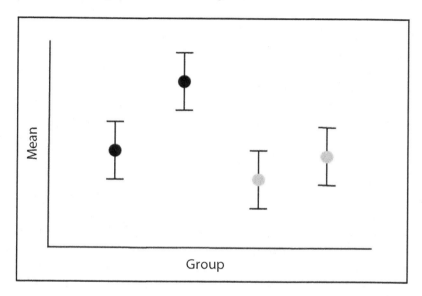

Fig. 2-3. Two hypothetical comparisons of means and 95% confidence intervals.
The 95% CIs around the means of the first two groups (indicated by black circles) do not overlap, indicating a significant difference between the means. The CIs around the means of the second two groups (gray circles) overlap considerably, indicating that the means are not significantly different from one another.

Nonsignificant Differences and Rare Events

If you conclude that there is no significant difference between the means of your samples, does that prove that the true parametric means of the two groups are equal?

No!

Remember that statistical analyses are based on the rare event rule. If two groups have equal means, then the samples we draw should be similar *most of the time*, and if two groups have unequal means, then *most* of the samples we could take should differ. Sometimes, though, sampling error causes unexpected things to happen. Rare events are not impossible; sometimes, for example, people win the lottery or are struck by lightning—sometimes twice. Whenever you conduct scientific studies, you should keep in mind that statistics cannot *prove* anything; they can only tell us how confident we are in our conclusions.

Testing Hypotheses about Frequencies

Not all ecological studies compare means. Sometimes you will instead be interested in how individuals are distributed among groups (i.e., you will want to compare frequencies). One of the clearest examples of this is in studies of Mendelian inheritance. If a particular trait exhibits simple dominance, and two heterozygotes mate, then we expect that 75% of their offspring will display the dominant phenotype. But what if we observe that 11 of their 16 offspring show the dominant phenotype? Or 10? We know that biological populations are inherently variable, so how different must our observations be from the expected results before we would conclude that our original assumption (simple dominance) was incorrect?

In ecology, there are many situations in which we face similar problems. We might want to know whether a species of spider is evenly distributed among three habitat types. We might want to test whether a population of rodents has a 1:1 ratio of males to females. We might want to know whether a particular bat prefers to eat one species of moth or chooses all moth species with equal frequency. Just as with comparisons of means, the possibilities are nearly endless.

Chi-Square Goodness-of-fit Test and Frequency Data

To answer this type of question, we will use a statistical technique called the *chi-square good-ness-of-fit test*. It provides us with an objective way to determine whether our observations are sufficiently different from our expectations to constitute evidence against our starting assumption (which we will hereafter call the *null hypothesis*). To conduct this test, you will need to have, for each group or category, two quantities: (1) the number of individuals that would be expected in the category if the null hypothesis is true, and (2) the actual number of individuals you observed. With these values, you can calculate the chi-square test statistic:

$$\chi^2 = \sum_{i=1}^{k} \frac{(\text{Observed} - \text{Expected})^2}{\text{Expected}}$$

This equation simply requires you to subtract the expected value from the observed value for each category or group, square the result, and divide by the expected value. Once you have done this for each category, add up all of those values (that's that the "Σ" means). If your null hypothesis is true—in other words, if the real world operates according to your initial assumption—then we should expect χ^2 to equal zero, plus some small variation due to sampling error. The more different the observed values are from the expected, the larger χ^2 will be. If it is large enough, we can conclude that the null hypothesis is probably false.

How large does χ^2 need to be? Statisticians have determined how the χ^2 statistic should behave if the null hypothesis is true, so we know how large it should get just as a result of sampling error. This "critical value" depends on the number of categories you're comparing. In general, the more categories you examine, the larger χ^2 must be to be considered evidence against the null hypothesis. This again is rooted in the rare event rule: if the null hypothesis is true, we can occasionally obtain observed values that are very different from the expected values, but this should happen very rarely. So if you obtain a set of observed values that is so extreme that it should be found 5% of the time or less when the null hypothesis is true, then you can conclude that the observed data are significantly different from your expectations—in other words, you can reject the null hypothesis. If you had such a case, your next job would be to determine what, biologically, would cause your null hypothesis to be false.

In Chapter 9, we provide more details on the mechanics of chi-square tests, as well as the critical values you will need to draw conclusions about hypotheses you will test in your field studies. We also present instructions for the calculation of your test statistics using Microsoft Excel, including a detailed example of the procedure.

KEY CONCEPTS TO REMEMBER:

- Biological populations are variable. The only way to be absolutely certain of our conclusions is to census the entire population, which is usually impossible.
- We can use a sample statistic to estimate a characteristic of the whole population.
- We can use statistics to conduct hypothesis tests based on the rare event rule: if our hypothesis suggests that a particular event should not occur, but we observe it anyway, then we can reject the hypothesis.
- Consequently, if our results are so different from what would be expected that it probably could not have happened by chance (sampling error), then we conclude there is a "significant" difference.
- Because rare events sometimes happen, we can never be 100% certain of our conclusions. In science, we never *prove* anything.

LITERATURE CITED

Julious, S. A. 2004. Using confidence intervals around individual means to assess statistical significance between two means. *Pharmaceutical Statistics* 3:217-222.

Leger, E. A., and K. J. Rice. 2003. Invasive California poppies (*Eschscholzia californica* Cham.) grow larger than native individuals under reduced competition. *Ecology Letters* 6:257-264.

Triola, M. M., and M. F. Triola. 2006. *Biostatistics for the Biological and Health Sciences*. Boston: Pearson/Addison-Wesley, 699 pp.

EXERCISE: POPULATIONS AND SAMPLING

Objectives:
1) **Practice the use of sub-sampling and sample statistics to understand variation among samples from a particular population.**
2) **Practice the use of spreadsheets to record and analyze sample data.**

Have you ever looked out over a field and wondered how many honey bees might be flying through the field and gathering pollen from flowers? Or maybe you have stood in the rocky intertidal zone at the seashore and wondered how many green crabs or common periwinkles were on the beach. How would you answer this kind of question? The amount of effort involved in counting all of organisms in such a large area would be overwhelming as well as too costly in terms of time and finances. So how could you get close to a truly representative answer without counting every individual? This is a problem that biologists encounter in doing many types of field or laboratory research. What do biologists do to try to answer the question, "How do we characterize some aspect of an entire population when we only have enough resources to study a small number of individuals?"

In Chapter 2 "Why do we use statistics," we presented the problems associated with sampling from populations and the value of using sample statistics to test hypotheses. Biologists have devised many methods that make it possible to take **samples** of a larger population and develop reasonable estimates and mathematical descriptions that characterize the entire population. Our practice investigation today will focus on learning the principles of sampling and how to take the data from the samples to characterize the entire population using descriptive and analytical statistics.

Fifteen-Bean Community
Our example population will be a container of dried beans from a 15-bean soup package. Each distinct color and size or shape of the beans represents a separate species of organism in our "bean community," and so there are 15 populations of organisms in our overall community. Our study habitat will be a white plastic tray that has been portioned into sections by drawing 3 rows and 4 columns inside the tray on the bottom. Our 15-bean community has "colonized" our tray. Our goal is to estimate the population size of individual bean species without counting every individual. We will characterize the results of our work using descriptive statistical measures known as the **mean, median, mode**, and measures of sampling variability known as the **standard deviation** and the **95% confidence interval**. We will use the functions within Microsoft Excel to help us calculate these values, so you will need to record your data in an Excel spreadsheet.

How and where do you sample from your population?
Organisms usually have preferences for where they like to live, determined by their tolerances of environmental conditions and their niche. As a result, species rarely are uniformly distributed over the area in which they live. This makes sampling a challenge because we want to be sure we do not introduce a bias into how we take samples to characterize our population. One way to avoid such a bias is to create a scheme that allows you to randomly select a location on a sampling grid or along a line transect. Because the sampling area in our tray has been partitioned into 3 rows and 4 columns, we can roll a die to select a number between 1 and 3 to select a row and then again between 1 and 4 to select a column. These two numbers become

cell reference locators to the cell or grid in our community tray to sample our organisms. Our goal is to sample 25% of the habitat to characterize the populations of the "green lentil bean" and the "small deep red bean" species. After you select the row and column coordinates of **three** grids in your tray, use a plastic spoon to remove all of the beans within your chosen grids. Count the number of beans for each bean species you find in each grid, and record your results on the attached data sheet. Use these data sheets to develop a spreadsheet to record data and do your calculations.

Shown below is an example of a 3 x 4 sample grid drawn in a white plastic tray. Cells for sampling are selected by randomly determining the column and row number to locate where to remove the "bean" organisms.

1-1	1-2	1-3	1-4
2-1	2-2	2-3	2-4
3-1	3-2	3-3	3-4

Density and estimating the total population size of species

Once you have sampled 25% of your bean community, calculate the sum and the mean number of each bean species per sample (grid) using the SUM and AVERAGE functions in Excel. This represents an estimate of the density of each bean species because it is expressed as an average number per standardized sample area (in this case, per grid in the tray). If this were in a field and you had a grid made of multiple 1-m^2 grids or a series of 24-m^2 plots, then it could be the average number per square meter. Each team member should use the average number per grid for the green lentil and small dark red bean species and turn in answers to the following questions by the end of the lab period. Include a copy of your spreadsheet showing the data and spreadsheet calculations.

1. Estimate the total population size of each of these two species in the entire bean community using your data on the average number per grid.
2. Compare your lab team's estimates for the entire population of these two species with the results found by the other research groups in your lab section.
   a) How similar are the estimates?
   b) Are there any estimates that are dramatically different from the rest of the groups?

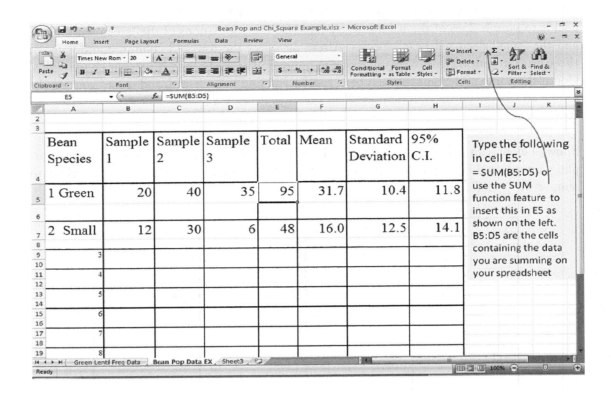

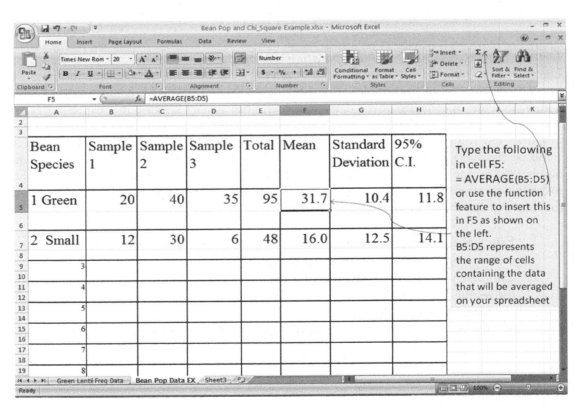

Variation and Confidence in your Sample Statistic

How much confidence do you have in your estimates of the average number of green lentil and deep red bean species? A quantitative estimate of confidence in a sample statistic like a mean is easier to compare rather than a subjective interpretation. One way to do this is to calculate a measure of the variability of the data used to calculate the average. Two measures commonly used to compare variation in data are the standard deviation and the 95% Confidence Interval around the mean. These can be calculated in Excel using the STDEV function and the CONFIDENCE function.

3. Use the STDEV and CONFIDENCE functions on the data you have collected and compare your 95% Confidence Intervals for the average number per grid (density) for the two bean species between the research groups in your lab section. Make a table showing the mean, standard deviation, and 95% confidence interval for the two species for each research group in your lab section.

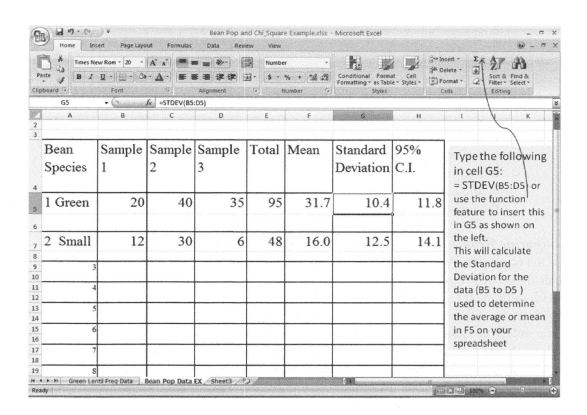

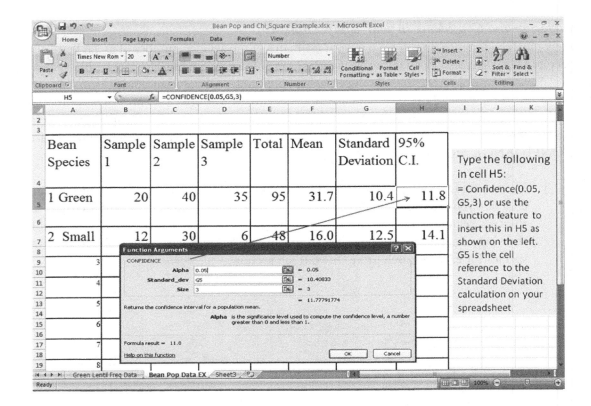

a) How do the values of the 95% Confidence Intervals relate to differences in the variability of the population estimates for these two species?

b) Discuss the meaning of the variation in the 95% Confidence Intervals calculated by the research groups in your lab section with your lab instructor and the rest of the members of your lab section.

Comparing frequency of occurrence data of organisms between locations

Use the count data you collected for your three sub-samples in estimating the green lentil and small dark red bean species as your data to measure the frequency of occurrence of these species in three distinct locations or habitats. Let's consider that each sub-sample represented a distinctly different location in our community. Our no difference hypothesis, also known as the null hypothesis, is that these two species occur equally throughout our study area and so there should be no difference in their individual frequency of occurrence between the three locations or habitats that we sampled. How could we test our hypothesis to see if our frequency data actually fits this expected pattern of occurrence? Biologists often try to examine questions like this about count data where each data point represents a whole organism or a distinct category rather than data that are continuous measures with values that can have decimal fractions between two whole units like temperature data. You can have a series of temperature values that could have decimal fractions of a degree but you can't have a fraction of an organism in a community and have it be living!

One of the hypothesis testing tools we use to study frequency of occurrence data in biology is the Chi-Square Goodness-of-Fit test. You want to see if the observed distribution of count data "fits" what you expected if there was no difference in their occurrence between habitats. See the example below of species occurrence data as an example of a Chi-Square calculation.

Use the data in the example below and develop a practice spreadsheet in Excel that gives you the same results. Use the ChiInv function and compare it to what you find in a table of Chi-Square values for the 0.05 probability level and degrees of freedom equal to 2.

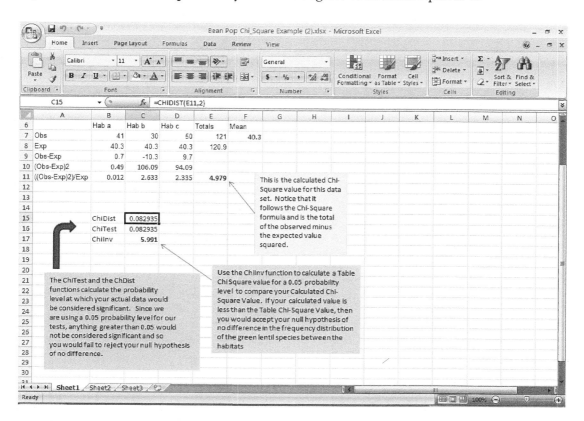

4. Now calculate a Chi-square value using your lab team's data set and compare your calculated value for your observed data to what is called a Critical Chi-Square value or Table Chi-Square value. Doing this will allow you to determine whether you will reject or fail to reject your no difference hypothesis about the frequency distribution of each species between the three habitats. Use the ChiInv function in Excel to calculate the exact Critical Chi-Square value to compare to your calculated Chi Square value or look it up in a Chi-Square Table. Discuss with your lab instructor how to use what is called the "degrees of freedom" (df = n − 1) to determine your Critical Chi-Square value.

Once you are confident of your ability to do this, create two separate tables where you substitute your own data for the green lentil and deep red bean species and calculate the expected values from your observed data in order to calculate the Chi Square value for each comparison. In each case, compare your calculated Chi-Square result to the Critical Chi-Square value. Discuss the results with your instructor. Complete the following questions and turn in your answers along with a copy of the spreadsheet you used to do these calculations:

a) Did you reject the null hypothesis of no difference in the frequency of occurrence of these two bean species? If so, then why? If not, then why not?

b) Did your results support or conflict with the findings of the other research teams in your lab section? Make a table showing how many research teams rejected or failed to reject the null hypothesis of no difference in frequency distribution for these two bean species.

ECOLOGY REPORT 1. TO BE TURNED IN AT THE END OF THE LABORATORY PERIOD. EACH STUDENT MUST TURN IN A REPORT.

FIFTEEN-BEAN COMMUNITY POPULATION DATA

Name:_____   Date:_____

Research Group Members:_____

Bean Species	Sample 1	Sample 2	Sample 3		Total	Mean	Standard Deviation	95% C.I.
1								
2								
3								
4								
5								
6								
7								

Bean Species	Sample 1	Sample 2	Sample 3		Total	Mean	Standard Deviation	95% C.I.
8								
9								
10								
11								
12								
13								
14								
15								
Mean								

C H A P T E R 3

Global Positioning Systems (GPS)

"Where am I?" This question has been asked by people throughout history. In the very beginnings of human history precise location was not overly important as long as our ancestors could find their favorite berry patch or water source. However, as civilization advanced, the need to find precise locations became more important. The classical Greeks and the early Chinese attempted to develop logical grid systems of the world, and the Roman geographer Claudius Ptolemaeus (known as Ptolemy) created a grid system and listed the coordinates for places throughout the known world in his book, *Geography*. During the Middle Ages, the modern system of latitude and longitude was developed and implemented. The need for an effective way to find a location on earth reached critical importance in 15th Century with the onset of the Age of Exploration, during which Europeans explored the world in search of trading partners and trade goods such as gold, silver, and spices. Western European explorers needed new, accurate maps, and the system of latitude and longitude provided the accuracy needed.

To understand this system, visualize the earth as a sphere or ball. Draw an imaginary line running around the circumference of the earth midway between the North Pole and the South Pole. This line is the equator, and it divides the earth into a northern hemisphere and a southern hemisphere. Next, imagine a series of lines drawn on the earth running from the North Pole to the South Pole, and another series of lines running around the earth parallel to the equator.

LATITUDE

On a globe or map, the lines that run horizontally are called lines of *latitude*. Latitude lines are also known as parallels because they are parallel to each other and to the equator. They are spaced at approximately equal distances; each degree of latitude spans approximately 69 miles (111 km). If the earth were a perfect sphere, this distance would be exact. But because the earth is an oblate ellipsoid (slightly egg-shaped), there is some small variation in the distance between parallels. A simple way of remembering that these parallel lines are called latitude is to visualize them as the horizontal rungs of a ladder ("ladder-tude"). Degrees latitude are numbered from 0° to 90° north and south. The equator is at 0°, the North Pole is at 90° north, and the South Pole is at 90° south.

LONGITUDE

The vertical lines are called longitude and are also known as meridians. Unlike lines of latitude, these are not parallel. They converge at the poles and are most distant from one another at the equator (about 69 miles or 111 km apart). By international convention, zero degrees longitude (0°) is located at Greenwich, England, the site of the British Royal Greenwich Observatory. The degrees continue 180° east and 180° west. In the Pacific Ocean, on the opposite side of the world from the Prime Meridian (0°), they meet and form the International Date Line. The Prime Meridian and International Date Line divide the earth in half from north to south to create eastern and western hemispheres, comparable to the way that the equator divides the earth into northern and southern hemispheres.

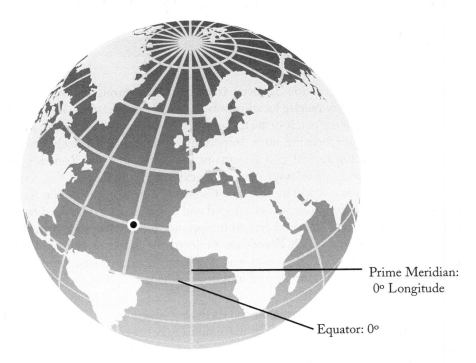

Fig. 3-1. A map of the earth displaying both latitude (including the equator) and longitude (including the Prime Meridian). A black dot inside a white circle indicates a location with the coordinates 30° N (latitude) and 30° W (longitude).

Thus, these two divisions, one by the equator and one by the combination of the Prime Meridian and the International Date Line, result in the earth being divided into four regions: a northern western quarter, a southern western quarter, a northern eastern quarter and a southern eastern quarter. The United States lies in the northern western quarter, China lies in the northern eastern quarter, most of South America lies in the southern western quarter, and the tip of Africa and Australia lie in the southern eastern quarter.

HOW LATITUDE AND LONGITUDE WORK TOGETHER

To precisely locate points on the earth's surface, degrees longitude and latitude have been divided into minutes (′) and seconds (″). There are 60 minutes in each degree and 60 seconds in each minute. Seconds can be further divided into tenths, hundredths, or even thousandths. For example, the Massachusetts State House in Boston is located at 42°21′31″N, 71°03′50″W (42 degrees, 21 minutes, and 31 seconds north of the equator and 71 degrees, 3 minutes and 50 seconds west of the Prime Meridian).

The GPS system of coordinates is based on the latitude and longitude system. To account for North versus South and East versus West, positive and negative numbers are used. Northern latitudes (north of the equator) are considered positive and southern latitudes are considered negative. All of our work in this course will be north of the equator, so you will not encounter negative latitude readings. A positive longitude is east of the Prime Meridian, and a negative longitude is to the west. In ecological field research, it is often necessary to use maps and record where you are sampling or observing populations and individuals. In the past, this often involved the use of landmarks and triangulation to locate the position with topographic maps or road maps. Today, the development of the civilian GPS system has greatly simplified locating positions in the field. The Global Positioning System (GPS) uses between 24 and 32 Medium Earth Orbit satellites that transmit precise microwave signals. These signals enable GPS receivers located on the ground to determine the current location of the receiver, as well as time, velocity, and direction of movement.

The GPS system was originally developed by the United States Department of Defense for military use, and is managed by the United States Air Force 50th Space Wing. The GPS system has been so successful and useful that several similar satellite navigation systems are proposed or in production, including the Russian GLONASS, the European Galileo positioning system, China's proposed COMPASS navigation system, and India's IRNSS navigation system. All of these systems will use Medium Earth Orbit satellites to locate positions on the earth's surface.

Because GPS was developed originally for military use, it was highly restricted. Then, in 1983, Korean Air Lines Flight 007 was shot down after straying into the USSR's prohibited airspace. As a result, President Ronald Reagan issued a directive making GPS freely available for civilian use. The first civilian versions of GPS receivers were purposefully less accurate and precise than military versions. Today, however, good civilian receivers with high accuracy and precision are available. Since it became available for civilian use, GPS has become a widely used aid to navigation worldwide. In ecology, it is very useful for precisely locating research sites and for map-making and land surveying. We will record and map the locations of our research sites using data collected using hand-held civilian GPS receivers.

GPS coordinates can be reported in up to three different formats, due to the variety of GPS hardware available from different manufacturers. This difference in reporting coordinates must be taken into account when using different GPS systems or major errors in pinpointing locations can occur. If more than one system is used, the GPS coordinates will need to be converted from one system to another. One of these systems (WGS84) is a completely decimal format that is employed with GIS systems and found in the more expensive higher-end GPS equipment. We will not be using this system in this course and therefore will not discuss it. The other two systems will be used in this course, and you will need to understand the systems and be able to convert coordinates from one to the other.

Deg/Min/Sec: This is the standard minutes/seconds translation of latitude/longitude that has been used for centuries. Many modern GPS units use this traditional format. This system is also used by many state GPS systems, including MassGIS, and by Google Earth. For both degrees of latitude and degrees of longitude, the format can be positive or negative. The earth is divided into four sections (N, S, E and W). N (North) indicates north of the equator. S (South) indicates south of the equator. E (East) indicates east of the prime meridian and W (West) indicates west of the prime meridian. East of the prime meridian is positive (E) and west of the prime meridian (W) is negative. In certain cases, south of the equator (S) may also be considered negative.

GPS: This system is becoming the standard for civilian GPS units, and the hand-held units you will be using in this course will use this system. GPS uses a mixed minutes/decimal format. All values are positive, and the hemisphere is indicated by standard abbreviations (N, S, E, and W). Minutes follow the degrees of the coordinates, and seconds are not used. Instead, minutes are subdivided into hundredths of minutes. Most of the better hand-held GPS receivers, including the ones you will be using in this course, use this system. These units thus give the GPS location as Degrees, Minutes and hundredths of minutes (DDD,MM.MMMM).

This means that the GPS coordinate system employed by most civilian GPS receivers cannot be directly used with the Deg/Min/Sec system found on most maps, the state GPS systems, and Google Earth unless you convert the coordinates. The GPS coordinate system must be converted to the Deg/Min/Sec system before you try to find your site using a state GPS system or Google Earth. A GPS conversion worksheet is posted on the course webpage. There are also a number of GPS converters available online, including the following:

http://www.jeepreviews.com/wireless-gps-coordinates/

http://www.tirolland.net/geo/gpsconverter.xls

http://www.fcc.gov/mb/audio/bickel/DDDMMSS-decimal.html

For example, from the top of Mount Washington in New Hampshire, we would get a GPS reading of N 44° 16.200′ and W 71° 18.201′. Note again that we do not have any seconds; instead, we have degrees, minutes and hundredths of minutes. We can use one of the online converters to convert this reading to degrees, minutes, and seconds so we can locate our position on the map using Google Earth or on a topographic sheet of the area. The converter gives us N 44° 16′ 12.02″ and W 71° 18′ 12.06″ for our location on Mount Washington. We then use the coordinates of North 44 degrees 16 minutes and 12.02 seconds and West 71 degrees 18 minutes and 12.06 seconds to find our location on the top of Mount Washington using Google Earth.

The latest versions of Google Earth can use either system of GPS Coordinates. Google Earth will accept several different ways of entering the data. The simplest way is as follows for our example of Mount Washington in New Hampshire.

        44 16.200n, 71 18.201w

Just enter this in the "Fly to" space and Google Earth will take you there.

We will do two exercises to help familiarize you with the use of GPS. Once you complete each of these exercises, check your results with your lab instructor to determine whether you have used the GPS receiver correctly and whether you have made the conversion and located the unknown location correctly.

EXERCISE 1. USE OF THE GPS RECEIVER

During the first field trip to Wyman Meadows to study macroinvertebrate diversity, you will use the GPS receiver to locate your two sample locations. Check your coordinates with your laboratory instructor to make sure you have accurately read the receiver and have the correct coordinates. After you return from the field, you should covert these coordinates and find your field locations on a map using MassGIS or Google Earth. You should show these maps to your lab instructor at the next laboratory meeting to determine how accurate you were.

EXERCISE 2. IDENTIFICATION OF UNKNOWN LOCATION ON A MAP USING MassGIS OR GOOGLE EARTH

You should complete this part between now and the next laboratory meeting and turn in your results next week to your laboratory instructor. Your instructor will give each student a unique set of GPS coordinates in the same format the GPS receiver uses: Degrees, Minutes and hundredths of Minutes (DD MM.MMM). These coordinates indicate an unknown location. Find and identify your site on a map using MassGIS or Google Earth. Turn in your results next week and check with your lab instructor to determine whether you have correctly determined the location. If you have not correctly located the unknown location, your instructor will tell you to try again. Once you have correctly found your unknown location, you will have satisfied this assignment. A list of unknown locations and the student assigned to each will be posted in the laboratory and on the course web page.

Sean King, Kyle Fisk, Connor Cummings

CHAPTER 4

Terrestrial Macroinvertebrates: Predators, Habitat Cues, and Biodiversity

OBJECTIVES:

Determine whether the total number of spiders and mantids and total types of predators are related to the total number of non-predatory insects found in two habitats. Determine whether there is a difference in invertebrate diversity between the two habitats.

INTRODUCTION

The local Conservation Commission and Natural Resources Trust are keenly interested in habitats that support local biodiversity. Populations of praying mantids, *Stagmomantis carolina*, have been observed in large numbers in some of the local preserves, and questions have been raised about their population as well as the impact they have on the biodiversity of local insects. An experimental investigation by Wilder and Rypstra (2004) has shown that a Chinese mantid species (*Tenodera sinensis*) would spend more time on habitats that had chemical cues from crickets and habitats having brightly colored images of flowers than in blank or "grass" control habitats. This suggests that insect predators use environmental cues to find better habitats in which to hunt for prey. The objectives of our investigation are to determine the number and types of insect predators in two distinct habitats in one of the local parks and to look for a pattern or relationship to the density and biodiversity of non-predator insects. If we are able to find any state-listed (rare) species, we will report these findings to the Natural Heritage and Endangered Species Program. This information will then be included in the state database and may be of value for the BioMap2 project
(http://www.mass.gov/dfwele/dfw/nhesp/land_protection/biomap/biomap_home.htm).

At the research site, there are fields that are in various stages of terrestrial plant succession. Within each field are several patches of distinct habitats of different plant types. The two primary habitat types we will study are fields of grasses mixed with milkweed and large patches of goldenrod with herbaceous ground cover. In this pilot study, we want to investigate the patterns of occurrence of spiders and praying mantids between the two habitats and the diversity of terrestrial macroinvertebrates within two habitat types. We will also need to test whether there is a difference in the abundance of these two types of insect predators and the dominant macroinvertebrates found in these habitats.

When you complete the study, you will use the data from the research teams in your lab section to report results in a short research memo to the local Conservation Commission.

METHODS

A. Collection of samples in the field

Each research team will need to define study plots within the two distinct plant habitat types at the study location. You will need to quantify the amount of area to sample within each plant habitat and will need to use measuring tapes, stakes and/or flagging to outline a square or rectangular area of 24 m². Based on the shape of the habitat area you are studying, you will need to choose one of the following configurations that best fits your habitat areas: 2 x 12, 3 x 8, or 4 x 6. Once you have established your plots, take a GPS reading within each one by using the GPS receiver provided. Record these readings on the data sheets provided for each plot at the end of this chapter. In addition, draw a map of the overall study area that shows the general location of each of your sample plots within the larger study area. The field sketch should give the approximate dimensions of the plot, drawn to relative scale. Make the map large enough to show major features in the overall study area, such as streams, fences, and roads, and show any significant landmarks close to the plot. Indicate on the plot any vegetation characteristics of the plot and the direction of magnetic north. Your field sketch should look something like Fig. 4-1.

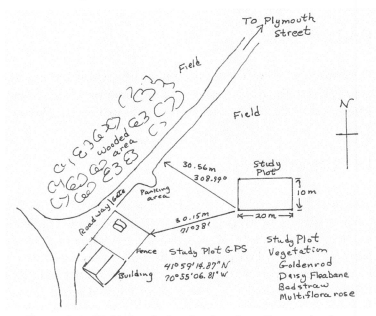

Figure 4-1. Field sketch showing location of a sample plot at Wyman Meadows.

For the purposes of this pilot study, we will focus on a subset of the invertebrate community that lives above the ground. They are relatively fast moving, which makes them difficult to capture and quantify. Additional species of macroinvertebrates live within the soil or at the base of the vegetation and will not be sampled in this pilot study. These other components of the macroinvertebrate fauna will have to be studied in the future in order to fully understand these ecosystems.

Figure 4-2. Measuring the sample plot using a metric tape

Figure 4-3. Sample plot is temporarily marked with biodegradable flagging.

After you have identified the plant habitats and marked the study areas, you will need to sample the macroinvertebrates that live above the ground level in order to compare the occurrence of species types and their densities. Use a sweep net to sample the insects in your study sites. To allow you to compare the data between sites, the sweeping procedure must be standardized. Any differences in the procedure from one site to another will bias the data and may lead to erroneous conclusions. Therefore, all individuals sweeping must take their samples in exactly the same manner. The standard procedure is outlined below.

Figure 4-4. The sample plot is swept with the collecting net to obtain the macroinvertebrate sample.

Before you actually sample your selected study sites, you should do a complete trial run of this entire procedure using an area outside of your study site as a test site. Go through the entire procedure. Although one person will be doing the sweeping, teamwork will be needed to successfully transfer the organisms from the net to the ziplock bag without any escaping.

You may capture some hornets, bees, or wasps. Be particularly careful when transferring these insects to the bag. Your research director will help you make the transfer of stinging insects if needed. You may also capture some praying mantises. Mantises are not a state-listed (rare) species. However, they are easy to identify, and therefore we do not have to collect them. Simply record the number of mantises you collected and release them outside of your study area.

Figure 4-5. All Praying Mantises collected are counted and then released unharmed.

We are using dry ice, instead of the poisons that entomologists often use for field collections, to immobilize and kill the macroinvertebrates. This approach is more environmentally friendly and will avoid exposing the members of our research team to toxic substances.

Sweep-netting procedure:
1. Use a heavy sweep net with muslin bag about 30 cm in diameter. Hold the net at arm's length at one side and take a series of **15** strong back and forth sweeps as you walk briskly along inside your selected habitat. Make the sweeps a full 180 degrees long and turn the net sharply at the end of each sweep so the insects stay trapped in the bag. At the end of your series of **15** sweeps, flip the bottom of the bag over the rim of the net to keep the insects trapped inside.
2. Select a Ziplock bag that is large enough to contain the entire net bag. Place a label inside the bag that has the habitat type, date, sample location, collectors' names, sample number, and lab section.
3. To remove the insects from the net, you need to be able to transfer them into the inside of the Ziplock bag. First close the bag of the net by tightly gripping the area above the bottom of the net bag with your hand. Then carefully invert the net bag inside the Ziplock bag. Make sure to do this quickly. It will help if one person keeps

the opening of the Ziplock bag closed while you invert the net and empty the contents into the Ziplock bag.

4. Repeat steps 1-3 so that you have **three samples of 15 sweeps each for each of the two habitat types.** This will give you a total of six Ziplock bags containing the samples.

5. Put these bags into a cooler with dry ice for 10 minutes or until they can be transferred into an ultra low temperature freezer.

6. The organisms should be stored in the collection bags in the laboratory freezer until counting. Group all the bags for each collection team with a large binder clip so they can be easily retrieved.

Figure 4-6. The collected macroinvertebrates are carefully transferred from the net to a plastic ziplock bag.

Figure 4-7. The plastic ziplock bag with the collected macroinvertebrates is labeled with the collector's name, research team number, date, and sample location.

Figure 4-8. The macroinvertebrates in the plastic ziplock bag are placed in a small field cooler with dry ice.

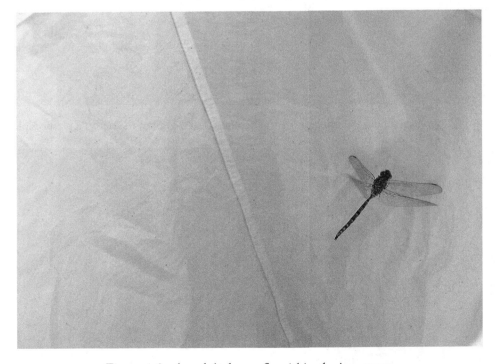

Figure 4-9. An adult dragonfly within the insect net.

For each sample plot, fill in the information on the data form at the end of this case study (CHAPTER 4 ASSIGNMENT 1 Field Assignment). This form must be turned in to the laboratory instructor at the end of today's field trip. Include your sketched map of your study area showing the recorded GPS readings for your two plots, the list of dominant vegetation, the total number of praying mantises and spiders found. List the common names of any macroinvertebrates you were able to preliminarily identify in the field for each site.

B. Identification and counting in the laboratory

The invertebrates should be left in the dry ice or freezer for at least a day before sorting and counting, and can be stored in the freezer for several weeks, if necessary. To speed up the sorting and identification process, each member of your team should take a separate subsample bag to sort.

1. Remove the bags and prepare a gridded white tray and plastic petri dishes for sorting the organisms from the vegetation debris.
2. Separate the invertebrates from the debris in each sample. Do this by placing the sample in a large white gridded plastic tray and using a dissecting scope or a binocular magnifier headset to see the invertebrates. Discard the plant material and place the invertebrates into one plastic petri dish labeled with the habitat type, sample number, and names of the research team members. **Ensure that each sample is placed in its own petri dish.**
3. Once all the invertebrates have been separated from the debris, sort the invertebrates into groups of morphologically similar individuals. To do this, place a sample in the white tray and sort the animals by shape, color, and patterns. Put like specimens together in the same cell or grid in the sorting tray. Ideally, you would like to have one species per grid cell, but because some insect species are very difficult to distinguish, we will sometimes have multiple species included in each "type."
4. Determine the number or species "types" and give each TYPE a unique letter (Species A, B, C, etc.). If a species type is considered a predator, put a mark in the column for Predators. You might conceivably use up the entire alphabet in "naming" your types. If you do, just start using two-letter names such as AA, AB, etc. Do this for the remaining samples for the same habitat so you have three columns of species groups. If you find the same type in more than one sample you should give it the same "name" (letter code). Try to line up similar species types from each sample with the same "name" (letter code) so they are alongside each other.
5. Count all the organisms of each type even though you have not yet identified any species. **Be sure that you use the same label for the same type in each sample!**
6. Record your totals for each type on the data sheet at the end of this chapter.
7. You will only need to identify the most abundant type in each habitat. Put these in separate plastic dishes with a unique label for each. Use insect keys provided and the lab reference collection and identify the dominant non-predatory species for each habitat.
8. If you are unable to get the exact species of the most abundant types, you should do the best you can to identify the specimens to the lowest possible taxonomic level using all the resources available, including consultation with the research director. **You will need to total ALL the organisms you found in each site.** This will include the total of the most abundant identified types and all the other types you found which were not identified to species or other taxonomic categories. For these unidentified types continue to use the letter designation originally given to them (A, B, C, etc).
9. Determine the total number of organisms, total number of predators, total types of predators (mantids and spiders), and the total number of non-predatory insects for each habitat. Obtain these same data from the other research teams in your lab section for writing your research memo.

Data Analysis

It is impossible to evaluate habitat preferences of predators without considering other species (many of which will be prey) in the community. Therefore, in addition to learning whether predators prefer one type of habitat over the other, we are interested in observing patterns of diversity. You should be able to identify several hypotheses about the relationship between predators and diversity. For example, predators might be attracted to habitats that contain a diverse array of prey items, or perhaps sites with high predator density have low diversity because predators have driven some prey species to local extinction. To test these hypotheses, we will need to calculate measures of diversity for each habitat.

Species Diversity

The number of species and the distribution of individuals within a community among species are often used as measures of community structure. The most useful measures of species diversity incorporate both the number of species (richness) and the distribution of individuals among species (evenness).

A community with high species diversity has many species with individuals that are relatively equally distributed among the different species or types. A community with low species diversity is composed of very few species (or types) or has a few species (or types) that are dominant and much more abundant than other species in the community.

The simplest measure of species diversity is the number of species (S) or the species richness. A number of diversity indices have been developed but one of the best is the index developed by Simpson (1949). Simpson's diversity index considers not only the number of species (S) and the total number of individuals (N), but also the proportion of the total that occurs in each species. Simpson showed that if you sampled a population and two individuals are taken randomly from a community, then the probability that the two individuals will be the same species is calculated by the following: (Brower et al., 1998).

$$l = \sum (n_i (n_i - 1)) / N (N - 1)$$

n_i = number of individuals of a given species

N = total number of individuals of all the species collected in that specific habitat or $\sum n_i$

This is considered to be a measure of **dominance** or concentration of N individuals among s species (Brower et al., 1998). Dominance is low for a collection of species with high diversity. Simpson diversity is calculated by either of the following formulas:

$$D_s = 1 - l \quad \text{or} \quad D_s = 1 - [\sum (n_i (n_i - 1)) / N (N - 1)]$$

This measure of the Simpson Diversity index assumes that the data are from a random sample from a community and that you do not have data from the entire community or sub-community (e.g., a laboratory culture of animals). See Brower et al. (1998) for modifications of the Simpson measure for data from an entire community or sub-community.

Table 4-1 presents a hypothetical data set showing how Simpson's Diversity index is calculated and interpreted. In this example, there were only three species found, and they were given the "names" (letter codes) X, Y and Z.

Table 4-1. Hypothetical data set of species numbers and abundance to illustrate the Simpson Diversity index.

Species, I	Abundance, n_i	Relative Density, $RD_{i \text{ or }} p_i$
X	60	60/95 = 0.632
Y	20	20/95 = 0.210
Z	15	15/95 = 0.158
$s = 3$	$N = 95$	

Using the data in Table 1,

$$D_s = 1 - [(60(59) + 20(19) + 15(14)) / 95(94)]$$
$$= 1 - 4130/ 8930$$
$$= 0.54$$

This value can be interpreted as the probability that two randomly selected individuals from the community would be of different species. A higher value of D_s therefore indicates a more diverse community (i.e., one that is less dominated by any one species).

Reporting Results

You should report your results in the format of a Research Memo to the local Conservation Commission. Your answers to the questions below and the graphs that you construct should help you to do so. Additional instructions for the production of a good Research Memo can be found in Chapter 7.

Individual Research Team Data

1. For each habitat, create a pie chart that shows the number of non-predatory species and the proportional abundance of each. You will use your count data for each species to construct these charts in Excel.
2. Construct a bar graph for each habitat showing the total number of insect predators(spiders and mantids) found in your sample, as well as the total number of predator types.
3. Using the pie charts based on total counts, determine which habitat has greater SPECIES RICHNESS and greater SPECIES EVENNESS.
4. Create a figure using Excel that compares the total number of non-predatory insects per 24 m^2 for the most abundant species ("types") from each habitat and the total number of insect predators found in each.
5. Describe the relationship between the total numbers of the most abundant non-predatory species and the abundance of insect predators. What is the ratio of total non-predatory insect species to the total number of predators in each habitat?
6. Are the same species dominant in each habitat? Are there any dominant species in common between the habitats? If so, how do the **total counts and relative densities** compare between the habitats?

7. Compare species richness and Simpson's diversity index between habitats. Does either measure of diversity differ between habitats? Do the two measures respond the same way to changes in habitat?

Entire Lab Section Research Team Data

8. Make a table that compares the Simpson Diversity between habitats for all the research teams in your lab section. Using the table of data for all the research teams in your lab section, decide which habitat generally has greater diversity? What do you think causes the differences in diversity? What evidence do you have that one habitat has greater diversity?

9. Compile the data from the other research teams in your lab section on the total number and types of predators in the two habitats, as well as their calculations on total number of individuals and total number of non-predatory insects they found in each habitat as well as the diversity (Ds). Use these data to calculate the average number of predators , the average total number of individuals, average total number of non-predatory insects and the Ds value in each of the two habitats. Discuss with your lab instructor and members of your lab section the interpretation of these average values between the two habitats.

10. Speculate on any habitat preferences observed for your top dominant species and the insect predators.

LITERATURE CITED

Brower, J. E., J. H. Zar, and C. N. Von Ende. 1998. *Field and Laboratory Methods for General Ecology*. 4th ed. WCB-McGraw Hill. Boston. 273pp.

Keefe, T. J., and E. P. Bergersen. 1977. A simple diversity index based on the theory of runs. *Water Research*. 11: 689-691.

Simpson, E. H. 1949. Measurement of diversity. *Nature* 163: 688.

Wilder, S. M. and A. L. Rypstra. 2004. Cues used in patch selection by praying mantis nymphs (Mantodea, Mantidae). *American Midland Naturalist* 153: 187-191.

TERRESTRIAL MACROINVERTEBRATE CASE STUDY DATA SHEET
COPY 2: PAGE 1
RESEARCH DIRECTOR COPY

Date: _____ Research Team (Base Group) Members: _____

Habitat Types: _A:_____   B:_____

Location:_____ Town: _____ State:_____

Sampler Type:_____ Size (cm): _____ Sweeps per Subsample: ___15_____

	Habitat A:			Habitat A	RD_i	Pred	Habitat B			Habitat B	RD_i	Pred
Species i	Sub 1	Sub 2	Sub 3	Sp Total (n_i)			Sub 1	Sub 2	Sub 3	Sp Total (n_i)		
A												
B												
C												
D												
E												
F												
G												
H												
I												
J												
K												

Species i	Habitat A:			Habitat A	RD_i	Pred	Habitat B			Habitat B	RD_i	Pred
	Sub 1	Sub 2	Sub 3	Sp Total (n_i)			Sub 1	Sub 2	Sub 3	Sp Total (n_i)		
L												
M												
N												
O												
P												
Total (Σn)												

TERRESTRIAL MACROINVERTEBRATE CASE STUDY DATA SHEET
COPY 2: PAGE 2
RESEARCH DIRECTOR COPY

Date: _____ Research Team (Base Group) Members: _____

Habitat Types: _A:_____ B:_____

Location:_____ Town: _____ State:_____

Sampler Type:_____ Size (cm): _____ Sweeps per Subsample: ___15_____

Species i	Habitat A: Sub 1	Sub 2	Sub 3	Habitat A Sp Total (n_i)	RD_i	Pred	Habitat B Sub 1	Sub 2	Sub 3	Habitat B Sp Total (n_i)	RD_i	Pred
Q												
R												
S												
T												
U												
V												
W												
X												
Y												
Z												
AA												

	Habitat A:			Habitat A	RD_i	Pred	Habitat B			Habitat B	RD_i	Pred
Species i	Sub 1	Sub 2	Sub 3	Sp Total (n_i)			Sub 1	Sub 2	Sub 3	Sp Total (n_i)		
BB												
CC												
DD												
EE												
FF												
Total (Σn)												

CHAPTER 4 ASSIGNMENT 2 LAB ASSIGNMENT WORKSHEETS

At the end of today's lab this sheet must be turned in to the laboratory instructor.

Research Team number _____ Date: _____
Names: _____
_____
_____
_____

Field Plot # 1

Species Counts for Field Plot # 1.

a		a a		b a		c a		D a		e a		f a	
b		a b		b b		c b		D b		e b		f b	
c		a c		b c		c c		D c		e c		f c	
d		a d		b d		c d		D d		e d		f d	
e		a e		b e		c e		D e		e e		f e	
f		a f		b f		c f		D f		e f		f f	
g		a g		b g		c g		D g		e g		f g	
h		a h		b h		c h		D h		e h		f h	
i		a i		b i		c i		D i		e i		f i	
j		a j		b j		c j		D j		e j		f j	
k		a k		b k		c k		D k		e k		f k	
l		a l		b l		c l		D l		e l		f l	
m		a m		b m		c m		D m		e m		f m	
n		a n		b n		c n		D n		e n		f n	
o		a o		b o		c o		D o		e o		f o	
p		a p		b p		c p		D p		e p		f p	
q		a q		b q		c q		D q		e q		f q	
r		a r		b r		c r		D r		e r		f r	

s		a s		b s		c s		D s		e s		f s	
t		a t		b t		c t		D t		e t		f t	
u		a u		b u		c u		D u		e u		f u	
v		a v		b v		c v		D v		e v		f v	
w		a w		b w		c w		D w		e w		f w	
x		a x		b x		c x		D x		e x		f x	
y		a y		b y		c y		D y		e y		f y	
z		a z		b z		c z		D z		e z		f z	

Top Species from Field Plot # 1

Field Plot # 2

Species Counts for Field Plot # 2.

		a		b		c		D		e		f	
a		a		b		c		D		e		f	
b		b		b		b		b		b		b	
c		c		c		c		c		c		c	
d		d		d		d		d		d		d	
e		e		e		e		e		e		e	
f		f		f		f		f		f		f	
g		g		g		g		g		g		g	
h		h		h		h		h		h		h	
i		i		i		i		i		i		i	
j		j		j		j		j		j		j	
k		k		k		k		k		k		k	
l		l		l		l		l		l		l	
m		m		m		m		m		m		m	
n		n		n		n		n		n		n	
o		o		o		o		o		o		o	
p		p		p		p		p		p		p	
q		q		q		q		q		q		q	
r		r		r		r		r		r		r	

s		a	s		b	s		c	s		D	s		e	s		f	s	
t		a	t		b	t		c	t		D	t		e	t		f	t	
u		a	u		b	u		c	u		D	u		e	u		f	u	
v		a	v		b	v		c	v		D	v		e	v		f	v	
w		a	w		b	w		c	w		D	w		e	w		f	w	
x		a	x		b	x		c	x		D	x		e	x		f	x	
y		a	y		b	y		c	y		D	y		e	y		f	y	
z		a	z		b	z		c	z		D	z		e	z		f	z	

Top Species from Field Plot # 2

C H A P T E R 5

Plankton Diversity Case Study

OBJECTIVES

Determine whether zooplankton prefer patches of water lilies over open water habitat during the day and whether they show a preference between two depths.

INTRODUCTION

You are a member of the state Department of Environmental Protection research team to investigate if freshwater zooplankton in shallow ponds prefer dense patches of water lilies during the day as a possible predator avoidance behavior. Preliminary reviews of past investigations reveal that zooplankton exhibit either diel vertical movement in the water column or diel horizontal movement away from the shore line in order to avoid visual predators like larger zooplankton, young of the year fish, and some aquatic insect larvae (Castro et al. 2007).

In the world of freshwater ecology in lakes and ponds, zooplankton play a major role as herbivorous grazers on phytoplankton (producers) and some act as predators on other zooplankton species. The size of their population, feeding rates, and distribution within a lake can have a major affect on phytoplankton population numbers, release of nutrients to the water, as well as the flow of energy to fish and invertebrates that feed on them. This interaction has been illustrated by the trophic cascade hypothesis developed by Carpenter and Kitchell (1993) and discussed by Molles (2008).

You will be investigating a shallow pond that has a rich growth of submersed, floating, and emergent aquatic plants. Zooplankton need to feed on phytoplankton and reportedly use aquatic plants to avoid being eaten by the many fish and invertebrate predators in the pond. In some cases, zooplankton will change their location daily to avoid predators and optimize feeding (Carpenter et al. 1987). As a preliminary investigation of the zooplankton in your study area, your research team will focus on whether there is a difference in the day-time habitat distribution of dominant zooplankton groups found in the pond. This will help us to determine if the dense cover of water lilies in the pond is serving as a refuge for zooplankton during the day.

Within the pond, there are several different shallow zones covered by water lilies, as well as deeper open-water zones. Our preliminary investigation will be limited to these two habitat zones of the pond. We will be need to sample within the open water area of the pond and within the area with water lilies in different parts of the pond. We want to know if there are different densities of total zooplankton and whether the same species are present at two depths within both habitat areas.

Figure 5-1. Small Pond suitable for the study of zooplankton distribution and diversity.

METHODS

A. Sampling Zooplankton and measuring Secchi Depths in the field

To study these organisms you need to construct a stable research platform. Each research team will use two canoes that have been bolted together in a catamaran-type design as a sampling platform on the pond. This greatly increases stability over a single canoe. Water safety regulations dictate that all team members must wear life jackets while working on the pond.

Once on the pond, each team will conduct two activities at each sampling site. First, you will use a Secchi disk to measure the depth of water transparency. Second, you will use a plankton net with 80-micron mesh and a battery-operated Shureflo Baitmaster pump with a weighted pickup hose to sample zooplankton from each site and depth. Since pumps vary in their performance, be sure to record the pump number your team uses. You will need an accurate estimate of the pump rate of your pump. Back at the lab, each research team will check the pump they used and determine the actual pumping rate for use in the calculation of zooplankton densities.

Figure 5-2. Two canoes held together with two-by-four lumber and bolts to form a stable catamaran sampling platform.

Figure 5-3. Two catamaran sampling platforms arriving at sampling sites.

Two water quality dataloggers will be deployed in the pond at two depths during the week of the investigation by collaborators from the Watershed Access Laboratory (WAL). These dataloggers will record water temperature, pH, and dissolved oxygen every hour so that you have information about the changes that occur in these physical and chemical factors. These data will be posted to the project website for your use.

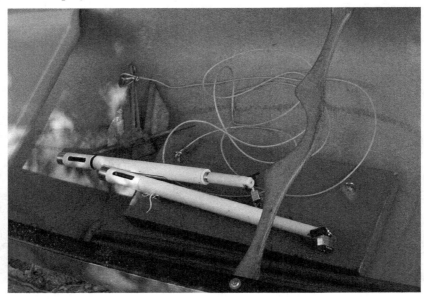

Figure 5-4. Datalogger ready for deployment in the pond.

Select two sites to compare within the pond. One should be an open-water site away from the data loggers, and the other should be just within an area of floating water lilies. Both sites must be at least 1.25 to 1.5 meters in depth. Be very careful to determine the depth first and make sure it is at least 1.25 meters deep before proceeding. The sample tube must never reach the bottom of the lake because mud will clog the pump. At each site, use an Aquascope while measuring the Secchi disk depth. Collect Secchi disk depths and zooplankton samples using the following procedures:

Figure 5-5. Deploying Secchi disk. Note the marks on the line represent 10 cm intervals.

1. Temporarily anchor your canoe/catamaran at the site so you can take your Secchi disk reading.

2. Put one end of the Aquascope below the surface of the water so you can view objects under the surface. Slowly lower the Secchi disk until it just disappears from view. Note the depth in centimeters. Raise the Secchi disk until it just reappears. Note this depth and average the two Secchi disk depth readings. This average is a crude estimate of the *compensation point*, which is the depth at which photosynthesis and respiration balance each other. This indicates the depth at which the oxygen level in the pond may change considerably. Above the compensation point on a sunny day, photosynthesis should dominate, leading to relatively high levels of oxygen. Below this depth, respiration should dominate, leading to lower levels of oxygen. Oxygen concentration may affect the species of zooplankton that will be found. Thus, the compensation point may be helpful for you as you interpret any differences in zooplankton abundance you detect between depths.

Figure 5-6. Using view glass and Secchi disk to determine depth of compensation point in pond.

3. Record the number of your battery-operated pump so you can later determine the correct volume of water you pumped through the Wisconsin Plankton Net. Fix the intake portion of the sampling hose on the marked rod at the desired sampling depth. Have a team member hold the rod against the side of the canoe so the pickup hose stays at the desired sampling depth.

4. Pull up your anchor just before you are ready to turn on your pump. Have someone on the team hold the net over the side of the canoe and place the discharge hose into the mouth of the net. Again, be very careful never to let the hose touch the bottom because this will suck mud into the net. Connect the pump to the gel battery and pump water through the net for 10 minutes while your boat slowly moves through your sample area.

Figure 5-7. The battery-operated Shureflo Baitmaster pump with a weighted pickup hose, used to sample zooplankton

Figure 5-8. The pump is used to pump pond water into the 80-micron mesh plankton net held between the canoes. Water is pumped for **10** minutes per sample while the boat slowly moves through the habitat.

Figure 5-9. Plankton sample is concentrated from the pond water as the water is pumped through the plankton net.

5. Use the wash bottle of distilled water to rinse plankton down the side of the net into the collecting chamber. Use distilled water for this washing so that you do not bias your sample by adding additional plankton.

Figure 5-10. Wash bottle is used to wash the net so that all the zooplankton ends up in the cod end of the net.

6. Remove the collecting chamber and empty its contents into a 250-ml HDPE sample bottle that is labeled with the site, date, depth, and names of the collectors. Use distilled water to rinse any attached organisms into the bottle. Use the 250- or 500-ml Nalgene graduated cylinder to determine the volume of the concentrated sample (in milliliters) and record the result on your data sheet and on the label for the sample bottle.

Figure 5-11. Concentrated plankton sample collecting in the cod end of the plankton net.

Figure 5-12. Preparing to transfer the plankton sample from the net to a sample bottle.

Figure 5-13. Transferring the plankton sample from the net to a sample bottle.

7. Preserve all samples with 70% ethanol (EtOH). The 250-ml HDPE sample bottle should be less than half full with sample. If it is not, split your sample between two bottles so that all sample bottles are less than half full. Then, add a volume of 70% EtOH to your sample that is equal to the volume of the sample.

8. Add three or four drops of Lugol's solution to each sample bottle. This is a stain that will make the zooplankton more visible under a microscope. The amount of Lugol's added is so small that you do not need to measure it.

Figure 5-14. EtOH is added to the plankton sample in the sample bottle.

Figure 5-15. A few drops of Lugol's solution are added to the plankton sample.

9. Make an additional label in pencil for each plankton sample. Put the sample site, specific location, depth, and date on each label, along with the names of your team members, and place it inside the sample jar.
10. Before taking the next sample, make sure to wash your net completely with pond water with the collecting chamber removed. Then give it a quick rinse with distilled water and reattach the collecting chamber.
11. Repeat steps 2-10 until you have collected all four samples.
12. Return to the laboratory with your samples. Make sure your samples are completely labeled and placed in a safe area of the laboratory designated by the laboratory director. It may be several weeks before you work with these samples, so make sure all necessary information is recorded and the samples are safely stored.

B. Checking the pumping rate of the plankton sampling pump

As mentioned earlier, the pumps deliver water at a rate of approximately 5-15 liters per minute. However, this is only an approximate rate. Each pump varies in its output, so you will need to determine the actual pump rate of your specific pump. Find the pump you used when you did your field sampling Set up your pump at the sink to pump water from one full bucket into an empty 1000ml Nalgene graduated cylinder. Have a team member use a stop watch and determine the time it takes to fill 1000ml. Repeat this two more times and calculate the average time it takes for the pump to deliver 1 liter. Now use this time to determine how many liters the pump will deliver in 1 minute. Since you pumped for 10 minutes, multiply the total volume pumped by 10 to get the amount of water pumped during your 10 minute sample period. If you pumped for a different time interval, you will need to adjust your mathematics accordingly to get the amount of water pumped per minute. Use this pump rate in your calculations to determine the amount of pond water that you sampled at each location. Record your pump rate in ml / minute.

C. Counting Zooplankton in the laboratory

Obtain a stereomicroscope with a mechanical stage, a Sedgewick-Rafter Cell with cover-slip, and a Hensen-Stempel Pipette. Check with your research director for access to these materials. In addition, you may need additional references for identification of zooplankton.

There are several zooplankton references available to use in the laboratory. One of the most useful is Pennak (1989), which has some excellent drawings. There are also some excellent online resources that you can access via the computers in the laboratory. One of the best is an excellent electronic zooplankton key available from the Center for Freshwater Biology of the University of New Hampshire. Use this key while you scan your sample to make preliminary identifications of the more abundant zooplankton. Have your lab instructor check your preliminary identifications.

>   http://cfb.unh.edu/

Several other useful websites include:
>   Freshwater Zooplankton
>   http://www.uv.es/~ciros/zoopl_en.html
>   Zooplankton in Freshwater
>   http://lakes.chebucto.org/zoo.html

Follow this procedure to prepare subsamples for analysis:
1. Invert the sample five times so it is uniformly mixed. DO NOT SHAKE the sample! Uncap the sample and immediately insert the Hensen-Stempel Pipette into the container with the plunger extending just beyond the end of the plastic barrel. Pull back on the plunger handle; this will randomly remove a 1-ml sub-sample. This procedure must be done quickly while the sample is still mixed.
2. Place a Sedgwick-Rafter Cell on top of a piece of paper towel on the lab bench. Position the rectangular cover slip diagonally across the cell so two corners are covered and two corners are exposed.
3. Hold the barrel of the pipette in one hand and steady it just above one of the open corners of the Sedgewick-Rafter Cell. With your other hand, SLOWLY push down on the handle connected to the plunger to empty the contents into the corner of the cell. The surface tension of the water in the sample should slowly turn the cover slip so the entire cell is covered. If you do not have exactly 1 ml of sub-sample, small depressions will form in each open corner and will form air bubbles. Try to avoid air bubbles by adding additional sample, but add only enough to fill the cell (i.e., no more than 1 ml).
4. Once the cover slip is in position and the bottom of the Sedgewick-Rafter cell is dry, place the cell on the mechanical stage of a stereomicroscope. Focus the microscope using the 10X objective. Use only the 10X objective for all your counting and identification; this will standardize data collection among all research teams. Follow the instructions below to count zooplankton in your subsample. Use the laboratory references and the online sources to identify these zooplankton to the following major taxonomic groups:

Copepoda: Rotifera
>   Cyclopoida or Calanoida   *Keratella sp.*
>   Copepod nauplii   *Kellicotia sp.*

Cladocera: Protozoa:
>   *Daphnia sp.*   *Ceratium sp.*
>   *Ceriodaphnia sp.*
>   *Bosmina sp.*
>   Chydorinae

There may be other dominant groups that appear in your sample. Use a silhouette picture of the organism and try to identify the specimen using the enclosed diagrams or refer to one of the suggested zooplankton keys. Consult with your project director on your identifications and record the numbers of each major type of zooplankton for the scans of the entire Sedgewick Rafter Cell.

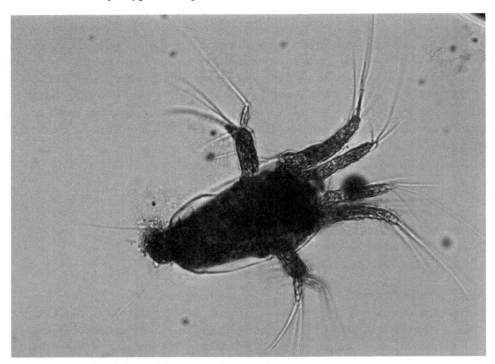

Figure 5-16. Example of immature copepod (copepod nauplius) typically found in freshwater ponds.

Figure 5-17. Cyclopoid copepod found in freshwater ponds.

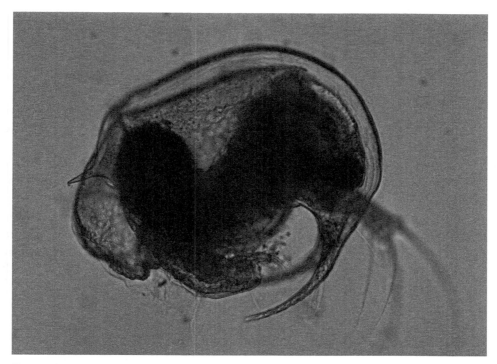

Figure 5-18. *Bosmina sp.* : a typical Cladoceran zooplankton found in freshwater ponds.

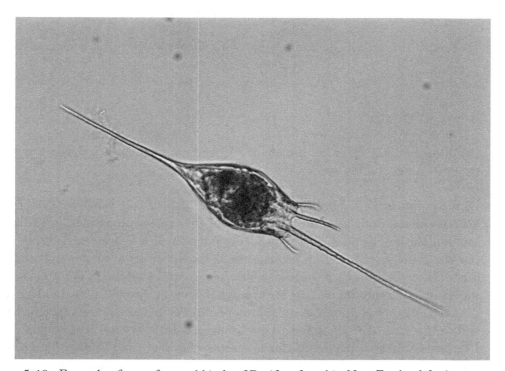

Figure 5-19. Example of one of several kinds of Rotifera found in New England freshwater ponds.

Enumeration of Zooplankton Density using a Sedgewick Rafter Cell (SR Cell)

1. **Record the concentrated sample volume on your data sheet. This is the volume you determined in the field before you added preservative to the sample.**
2. Use the mechanical stage on your microscope and scan across the entire length of the SR Cell. Systematically move your slide across the bottom to scan the entire edge,

move the slide up a bit so that you do not overlap what you already scanned, and move across that "strip" of the slide. Continue this until you cover the entire slide. Be sure to occasionally "focus through" your slide, especially if you see anything of interest that is slightly out of focus, as you are looking at a three-dimensional image. This will assure that you search the entire 1 ml sample. If your sample is too dense (i.e., there is a lot of phytoplankton keeping you from identifying zooplankton), you may wish to dilute your sample some more. Pour the slide contents back into your bottle, dilute your sample, and record the new sample volume.

3. Record your counts for each organism in the column provided on your data sheet. Prepare two additional slides and count zooplankton on these as well, for a total of three separate 1-ml subsamples per sample bottle.

4. Create an Excel Spreadsheet similar to the lab data sheet to record your counts. Download the zooplankton spreadsheet posted on the Blackboard site to convert your results from number of individuals per 1 ml to the **number of individuals per liter** of pond water. Consult with your lab instructor on how to use this spreadsheet. Cell formulas in the spreadsheet are based on the following for converting the data:

$$\text{Organisms per liter of lake water} = \frac{\text{Total Number of Organisms per 1 ml of sample X 1000}}{\text{Concentration Factor}}$$

$$\text{Concentration factor} = \frac{\text{Volume of Lake Filtered (ml)}}{\text{Volume of Concentrate (ml)}}$$

Volume of Concentrate = the total volume of the filtered sample before adding preservative

Volume of Lake Filtered (ml) = Pump Rate (ml/min) x Pumping Time (min)

(1 liter = 1000 ml)

Do this for each of the three dominant zooplankton types at each depth and at both the open water and lily pad sites.

5. **Estimate the average number of organisms per liter of lake water for each specific habitat and depth by calculating the mean of your three subsamples. Calculate the standard deviation and the 95% confidence interval (95% CI) for each average.**

6. Use the Excel spreadsheet to calculate the **average number of total zooplankton per liter of lake water for each specific habitat and depth** by totaling the counts for each sub-sample and then calculating the average of your three totals. This should give you the average number of total zooplankton per liter of lake water for a specific habitat and depth. Calculate the standard deviation and the 95% confidence interval (95% CI) for this average. Repeat this for each remaining depth and habitat. Each research team within a lab section must send a copy of their spreadsheet data to your lab instructor. These data will be posted on the course website and should be used in answering the following questions for your lab section.

7. Plot your results for the **average number of total zooplankton per liter of lake water** as outlined on the next page. Show the 95% CI as an error bar on your plankton graphs using Microsoft Excel. Discuss the trend observed in zooplankton numbers and distribution between the open water and lily habitats, and depths. Include these graphs and the table and plots of your probe data on dissolved oxygen, temperature

and pH and the table of the Secchi disk depths as your findings in the Research Memo to the Massachusetts Division of Fisheries. Give a conclusion about the project objective based on your data.

Plots to Make and Questions to Answer in Your Research Report:

1. Plot the **average number per liter** for each of the three most abundant zooplankton species at the two depths within a given site. (One Figure per site showing data for both depths). Is the **average number per liter** for each of the three dominant zooplankton equal **within** each site and depth? If not, then which one is most abundant and at what depth for that site? Is the same zooplankton group the most abundant at both depths within a given habitat?

2. Is the **average number per liter** of the total zooplankton **equal at the two depths for a given habitat?** If not, then does the average abundance increase or decrease with depth? How do the 95% confidence intervals compare for the average total zooplankton between the two depths?

3. Is the average number per liter for total zooplankton equal **between the two habitats at the same depth?** How do the 95% confidence intervals compare for the average total zooplankton between the two habitats?

4. Download the water quality data posted on the Blackboard site. Make a table of the average, maximum, and minimum values for the dissolved oxygen, pH, and temperature data for the two depths during the study period. Make a separate line graph for each of these parameters showing the hourly data for both depths on the same graph. Are there any differences in these water quality parameters between the two depths over the entire time of the study?

5. Make a table showing the average Secchi disk depth your team recorded for each habitat. Include the average Secchi disk depths for the other teams in your lab section and calculate the average for each habitat.

Testing Null Hypotheses about Total Zooplankton Distribution

Because you are comparing average total zooplankton data per liter of lake water between depths and habitats, compare the averages and the 95% CIs as outlined in the chapter on statistics in this lab manual. Do the 95% CI error bars overlap each other? Discuss with your lab instructor how you can use these data to evaluate the following **null hypotheses:**

1. There is no difference in the **average number** of total zooplankton per liter **between** the two depths within a given site.

2. There is no difference in the **average number** of total zooplankton per liter **between** the two habitats at the same depth.

You should do these tests of the null hypotheses using your research team's data and compare them to the results found by the other research teams in your lab. Do you reach the same conclusions with your data as the other research teams in your lab section? Discuss the result of this comparison with your lab instructor and the rest of the lab members.

LITERATURE CITED

Ambrose, H. W. A. III., K. P. Ambrose, D. J. Emlen, and K. L. Bright. 2007. *A Handbook of Biological Investigation*, 7th ed. Hunter Textbooks, Inc., Winston-Salem, NC.

Carpenter, S. R., and J. F. Kitchell. 1993. *The trophic cascade in lakes.* Cambridge University Press. Cambridge, England.

Carpenter, S. R., J. F. Kitchell, J. R. Hodgson, P. A. Cochran, J. J. Elser, M. M. Elser, D. M. Lodge, D. Kretchmer, X. He, and C. N. von Ende. 1987. Regulation of lake primary production by food web structure. *Ecology* 68: 1863-1876.

Castro, B. B., S. M. Marques, and F. Gonçalves. 2007. Habitat selection and diel distribution of the crustacean zooplankton from a shallow Mediterranean lake during the turbid and clear water phases. *Freshwater Biology.* 52:421-433.

Eckblad, J. 1992. *Laboratory Manual of Aquatic Biology.* Wm. C. Brown Publishers. Dubuque.

Molles, M. C. 2008. Ecology, Concepts and Applications. 4th ed. WEB/McGraw Hill. Boston.

Pennak, R. W. 1989. *Fresh-water Invertebrates of the United States.* 3rd ed. John Wiley & Sons, Inc. New York.

Ward, H. B., and G. C. Whipple. 1966. *Fresh Water Biology.* 2nd ed. John Wiley and Sons, Inc. New York.

Wetzel, R. G., and G. E. Likens. 1991. *Limnological Analyses.* 2nd ed. Springer-Verlag. New York.

DATA SHEET 1, COPY 1.   RESEARCH TEAM COPY
NET PLANKTON ANALYSIS - SEDGWICK RAFTER CELL

Lake:_____ Habitat: ____Open Water____Lilies Date:_____Pump #:____

Sample Number:_____
Total Volume Filtered by Net and Pump(ml): Depth 0.2 m_____ Depth 1.0 m_____

Concentrated Sample Volume Before Preservative (ml): 0.2 m_____ 1.0 m_____

Net Size: _____ Pump Rate (liters/min):_____
Concentration Factor: 0.2 m_____ 1.0 m_____

Collected By:_____

Plankton Counts (Three 1 ml Subsamples per Sample Bottle)
Research Team (1 ml) Depth: 0.2 m

Organism	Sub 1	Sub 2	Sub 3	Num. per liter 1	Num. per liter 2	Num. per liter 3	Avg Num. per liter	SD of Num. per liter	95% CI of Num. per liter
Copepod Nauplii									
Cyclopoid Copepod									
Calanoid Copepod									
Ceriodaphnia sp.									
Bosmina sp.									
Kellicotia sp.									
Kerratella sp.									
Brachionus sp.									
Ceratium sp.									
Other									
							Avg Total per L	SD of Total per L	95% CI
TOTALS									

DATA SHEET 1, COPY 2. RESEARCH TEAM COPY
NET PLANKTON ANALYSIS - SEDGWICK RAFTER CELL

Lake:_____ Habitat: ____Open Water____Lilies Date:_____Pump #:_____

Sample Number:_____
Total Volume Filtered by Net and Pump(ml): Depth 0.2 m_____ Depth 1.0 m_____

Concentrated Sample Volume Before Preservative (ml): 0.2 m_____ 1.0 m_____

Net Size: _____ Pump Rate (liters/min):_____
Concentration Factor: 0.2 m_____ 1.0 m_____

Collected By:_____

Plankton Counts (Three 1 ml Subsamples per Sample Bottle)
Research Team (1 ml) Depth: 1.0 m

Organism	Sub 1	Sub 2	Sub 3	Num. per liter 1	Num. per liter 2	Num. per liter 3	Avg Num. per liter	SD of Num. per liter	95% CI of Num. per liter
Copepod Nauplii									
Cyclopoid Copepod									
Calanoid Copepod									
Ceriodaphnia sp.									
Bosmina sp.									
Kellicotia sp.									
Kerratella sp.									
Brachionus sp.									
Ceratium sp.									
Other:									
							Avg Total per L	SD of Total per L	95% CI
TOTALS									

C H A P T E R 6

The Intertidal Invasion:
A Field Study of Invasive Species
And Intertidal Zonation

OBJECTIVES

1) Compare the distribution of four invertebrate species across the intertidal zone. 2) Use historical data and published literature to evaluate any changes or trends in population density of these species. 3) Learn how to analyze data and report results following a scientific journal format used in ecology.

INTRODUCTION

As humans began their colonization of the globe, they took with them a number of other species. Originally these included their commensals (e.g., dogs, goats, and pigs) and stowaways like rats. These animals integrated into the new ecosystems they encountered, often with unpredictable and harmful effects. Ecosystems worldwide changed dramatically due to these invasive species. In recent years, the impact of invasive species has intensified as new species have been purposely introduced by unwise humans or have serendipitously hitched rides on commercial shipping or been imported along with wood products and food.

The term "invasive species" is used in several different ways in the ecological literature. The most common conception applies the term to non-native species of plants or animals that have adverse economic or ecological effects on the habitat that they have colonized. This is the view of invasive species most commonly used by government organizations and conservation groups. Sometimes the term is used in a broader sense to include both native and non-native species that achieve very high densities in a particular habitat. Finally, some authors expand the definition even further to define an invasive species as a widespread non-indigenous species. This last definition does not require that the invasive species do harm, but simply that it colonizes new habitats.

An invasive species can impact an ecosystem in several ways. Often, studies of invasive species focus on competition. This is because many invasive species appear to have specific traits or combinations of traits that enable them to out-compete native species. For example, some invasive species grow or reproduce more rapidly than their native counterparts, can tolerate a wider range of environmental conditions (Kolar and Lodge 2001), or might have few natural enemies in their new habitat and therefore be less constrained by predation or parasitism than their competitors. In addition, invasive species often prey on native species in large numbers (e.g., Bourdeau and O'Connor 2003). Thus, an all-too-common outcome of the appearance of an invasive species in a habitat is a decline or even disappearance of native species.

Your ecological consulting laboratory has been hired to investigate the spread of the Asian shore crab, *Hemigrapsus sanguineus*, an exotic invasive species in the intertidal zone of the state. This species has already had an impact on algal and invertebrate populations within the intertidal zones of other New England states (Bordeau and O'Connor 2003). To understand the possible impact of this invasive species, you must develop a model of how intertidal organisms are distributed and the major factors that determine their distribution.

Interactions between species and with their physical, chemical, and geological environment can determine how species are distributed along an ecological gradient. The marine intertidal zone is a unique ecosystem where we can observe species distribution patterns along a gradient of environmental factors. The distribution of a particular species is related to its tolerance of physical and chemical changes that occur as the tide changes daily and seasonally, as well as to biological interactions between species. Where an organism lives determines how long it will have to withstand exposure to air and to what degree it will have to tolerate changes in air temperature and other weather conditions (Little et al. 2009). Thus, the spatial distribution of a species can provide a great deal of information about its tolerance limits and, potentially, its competitive ability.

You will conduct a study of the distribution of four species in the intertidal zone. Compare your results to the data collected in previous years posted on the course web site to evaluate how the Asian shore crab might be affecting population size of the three other species. Your research director has requested that you submit your results in the format of a scientific paper suitable for submission to a major ecological journal.

Figure 6-1. Beach at low tide showing exposed intertidal zone

SAMPLING TO DISCOVER PATTERNS OF SPECIES DISTRIBUTION

Sampling species along an environmental gradient can help us understand aspects of their ecology and why they occur in particular distribution patterns in an ecosystem. Understanding these patterns will help us to understand how the Asian shore crab is affecting the coastal zone ecology. To develop our model, we will need to collect data and analyze patterns of species distributions. Following the format recommended in Ambrose et al. (2007) for establishing a **null hypothesis (H_o)**, we will begin with the simplest possible assumption about the distribution of species and assume there is no difference in abundance of four intertidal invertebrate species at three sites on a sampling line (transect). The transect will **start** at the normal high tide mark closest to the beach and **end** at the low tide mark or open water edge for the day of our field trip. Since tides are influenced by the gravitational effects of the moon and sun on the earth, the height of the high tide and low tide will vary with the lunar cycle and with season. Consult your textbook for more background information on tides and the intertidal ecosystem.

In consultation with the research director, we have developed a research protocol to gather the data to test our null hypothesis. Each field team of three or four students will work along a transect starting from the high tide mark and working toward the low tide line of the intertidal zone. Each team needs to sample the selected invertebrates in the intertidal zone at the same distances. The research director has determined that at the research beach site the best sampling locations will be at **20m, 35m, and 50m** distances **measured from the high tide level** within your study area. For simplicity, we can code these areas as follows: 20m = high beach, 35m = mid-beach, and 50m = low beach. Final transect locations will be determined by your lab teams in consultation with your research director.

1. To compare data collected by different research teams, everyone must use standard sampling techniques. We are using standardized circular field samplers that are 76.2 cm in diameter. Determine the area of the sampler ($A = \pi r^2$) before the next lab meeting.
2. To help you correctly choose your sample locations, use a metric tape measure to measure the distances ***FROM THE HIGH TIDE LINE*** and mark each of your locations with a stake.
3. At each of the three sampling distances, you will establish your study plots by placing four circular samplers in a square pattern around the stake (Fig. 6-2). Each one of the four sample plots at each distance is called a sampling *quadrat* (not to be confused with a quadrant). Often these are four-sided, but we are using a circular one in this study.

UPPER BEACH

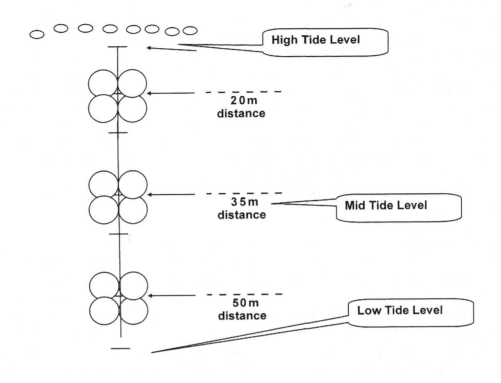

OCEAN

Figure 6-2. Diagram showing sampling quadrats set at the
three sampling distances along the beach profile.

Figure 6-3. Beach at low tide showing students setting up their transects.

4. We will only have enough time and money to sample three out of the four quadrats at each distance. Therefore, you must use a die, random number table, or some other means to randomly eliminate one of the four quadrats, leaving three to sample.

5. Place your sampler over each selected sector and, for each species listed on your data sheet, count the number of individuals inside the sampling frame. ***Count live individuals only. Do not count the shells of dead animals.*** The research director has determined that we will only be able to count four species within our budget and time allocation. We will concentrate our efforts on the common periwinkle (*Littorina littorea*), blue mussel (*Mytilis edulis*), green crab (*Carcinus maenus*) and the Asian shore crab (*Hemigrapsus sanguineus*). The Asian shore crab is the exotic invasive species that is of concern to our client. It has been in the Mid-Atlantic coast area since 1988. Use the information in Gosner (1979) and the illustrations in Figs. 6-4 to 6-10 as aids to identify each of these species.

Figure 6-4. The invasive Asian shore crab.

Figure 6-5. The green crab.

Figure 6-6. The green crab and Asian shore crab together.

Figure 6-7. Periwinkles.

Figure 6-8. Periwinkles on rocks within intertidal zone.

Figure 6-9. Blue mussels.

Figure 6-10. Blue mussels attached to the rocks within the intertidal zone.

Record the species count data for each sample separately. See Table 1 for an example of how data for the three randomly selected grid sectors at the 20m distance would be recorded for the three quadrats. Repeat the procedure at each of the selected sampling distances.

Figure 6-11. Four identical samplers in place at mid-beach location on the intertidal zone transect.

Figure 6-12. One of the samplers has been randomly removed, leaving three in place at mid-beach location on the intertidal zone transect.

Figure 6-13. Carefully count all the individuals of the four target species. Organisms can be placed temporarily in a plastic bag until all are counted. Then the organisms are returned to their habitat.

Figure 6-14. Students working at sample locations within the intertidal zone.

QUANTITATIVE MORPHOMETICS

As you collect and count your specimens for each of the three locations along the tidal gradient, place the animals in plastic bags. This will prevent counting the same animal more than once and will provide the sample group for this part of the investigation.

After you have collected all animals from each sample area, take the 10 largest animals from each species and measure their size using the measuring template provided. This measuring template allows you to measure the animals in millimeters (mm).

Take the following measurements:

For periwinkles – bottom of shell to the top of the spire
For the Asian shore crab – maximum width of the carapace
For the green crab – maximum width of the carapace
For the blue mussel – maximum length of the shell

Record this information on the data sheet provided for this purpose.

Data Reporting
Carefully record your data on the data sheets provided. In addition, you must record your raw count data on the sheet labeled "**Field Report Sheet.**" Note that this sheet also has a place for you to report the diameter of your sampler. Make sure this sheet is complete and correct and that the diameter of the sampler is reported. Each research team **MUST turn in** this sheet to your lab instructor before leaving the beach study area.

Beach Stewardship
As part of your understanding of ecology, you need to begin to appreciate the impact that humans are having on the earth and what you can do to help even in very small ways. Once your Research Team has finished with the data gathering, you will be given a bag in which to collect beach debris. This material will be brought back to the campus, sorted and cataloged, and then either recycled or disposed of in a proper manner. The data from the beach cleanup will be shared with the class so that you can gain an appreciation of the nature of marine debris. Marine debris is a major environmental problem, as it causes direct and indirect mortality to marine organisms and has a negative impact on marine ecosystems.

Data Analysis
There are two basic types of data: Continuous Data and Discrete Data. The count data that you acquired in this case study are discrete data. You counted 10 or 20 or some discrete number of organisms. You did not find 12.25 periwinkles. There are particular statistics, including chi-square, which can be legitimately used in the analysis of discrete data sets like this. However, low expected values make chi-square tests unreliable. For this reason, we will be using both the research group and class data to see how results can change if you look at a larger data set.

The other kind of data is continuous data. If the distribution of these data is graphed, there would be no breaks like we would find with discrete data. It is possible to convert discrete data to continuous data. For example, we can convert the count data from our circular samplers to continuous data (density) by converting the data to the number of organisms per square meter. The data can then be analyzed using statistical treatments appropriate to continuous data sets, such as the 95% confidence interval approach you used in previous case studies. With continuous data it is possible not to have whole numbers. For example, we may find that we have an average of 23.34 green crabs per square meter at the low tide sample site.

For this case study, you should analyze the data using both a continuous data approach (mean ± 95% CI; Part A below) and a discrete data approach (Chi-square goodness-of-fit test; Part B below) and compare the result between the two approaches. Answer the questions in each section below to discover what each of these data analysis approaches reveals about these four species in this intertidal zone.

Analysis of Data to Investigate Trends:

At the completion of the lab, you will have recorded the results for your research team on the *Individual Research Team Lab Sheet*. There are two copies of this form. One copy is for your research team to keep for your records, and the other must be given to your laboratory instructor. The laboratory instructor will compile the data from all research teams and post the data on the class web site. This combined data set will be the "class data set."

Lab Calculations Week 1 Part A: Density Data (mean ± 95% CI)

1. **Convert each species count to density of organisms per meter square (m²)** by dividing the species count by the area of the sampler in square meters. Express the results as number per m².

    To do a statistical analysis of the data set to test the null hypothesis, you will need to convert both your research team's raw count data and the combined research project raw count data into density data. You will have two sets of density data: one for your research team and one for the class data set. Use the Excel spreadsheet to do this conversion.

2. **Sum and Average the density data for each species**
    Using the *species density data*,
    A) Calculate mean density, standard deviation, and a 95% confidence interval around the mean for each species, *using the three samples your research team collected at each sample distance.*
    B) Using the class data set, calculate new values for mean density, standard deviation, and a 95% confidence interval around the mean for each species at each sample distance. *These data can be found on the course web page.*

3. **Use Bar Graphs to Display Patterns and Trends**
    Your laboratory instructor will demonstrate how to analyze the data using error bars in Excel for testing the null hypothesis. You will need to bring your **Count Data and Density Data** to the laboratory meeting.
    You will need to organize your data to do the following:
    A) Using your individual Research Team data, *plot a bar graph of the average density of EACH of the FOUR species at all three distances. (This will result in a total of four graphs, one for each species; each graph should be saved as a separate sheet in Excel.) Make sure to label the tab at the bottom of each section of Excel as you proceed so you can identify each graph and data set once you are finished with the analysis.*
    B) Plot an additional graph for each species, using the average density based on the class data set (data from all research teams as posted on the course website).

Lab Calculations Week 1 Part B: Count Data Approach (Chi-Square Analysis)

1. **Sum and Average the count data for each species**
   Using the *species count data,*
   A) Calculate the *total sum* and *mean for each species for the three samples your research team collected at each sample distance.*
   B) Calculate the total sum and mean for each species at each distance based on the class data set (data from all research teams from the entire class posted on the course website).

2. **Use Bar Graphs to Display Patterns and Trends**
   You will need to organize your count data to do the following:
   A) Using your individual research team data, *plot a bar graph of the pooled count data for EACH of the FOUR species between the three distances. (Total of Four Graphs)*
   B) Plot an additional graph for each species, using the class count data set.

Lab Calculations Week 2

Questions to Answer in Your Research Report:

1. Using your individual research team data, is the average density for each species equal within each sample site? If they are not, then which one has the greatest average density (most abundant)? Which one is least abundant? Which species has the greatest variation (standard deviation) in density data? Which one has the greatest 95% confidence interval?

2. Using your individual research team data for each species, compare average density between the three sample distances from the high tide mark. Does the average density increase or decrease as you get further from the high tide mark? What is the trend for all four species? Do all species show the same trend?

3. Do the same analysis using the class data set. Does the trend change for any of the four species when you use the class data set (data from all the research teams for the entire class combined)?

4. Do the trends you found using your team's data differ from the trends found for any of the four species when you used the class data set (combined count data from all the research teams in the entire class)?

Testing Null Hypotheses about Species Distribution Count Data Using Chi-Square

Statistical analysis of count data using chi-square requires that no expected value is equal to zero and no more than 20% of the expected values are less than five. To meet the requirements of this type of test, your laboratory instructor has made the decision to pool your research team's raw count data with those of the rest of the research teams before proceeding with the analysis of frequency data using chi-square. Thus, for this analysis you will be using the class data set only.

Use the Chi-square goodness-of-fit test outlined in Ambrose et al. (2007) and Chapter 9 to test whether you should reject the following **null hypotheses** for the class data set (pooled count data):

1. There is no difference in the **Count Data** for each of the species **within** each sample distance. (Chi-square goodness-of-fit test) (Three tests).

2. There is no difference in the **Count Data** of a particular species **between** the three sample distances. (Chi-square goodness-of-fit test) (Four tests).

The laboratory instructor will go over these analyses and statistics and discuss the use of the chi-square goodness-of-fit test. Chapter 9 contains a detailed example of how chi-square can be used to test the null hypothesis using data from this research project.

Calculation Tips and Conventions for this case study:
1) When you are calculating chi-square values, always retain 4 decimal places in your mathematical operations.
2) Round your calculated chi-square value to 3 decimal places when you have totaled and have the final value since chi-square tables use 3 decimal places.

Quantitative Morphometrics

You measured the body size of the four species at plots in the high, middle, and low intertidal zones. Based on characteristics of the physical environment and your understanding of the basic biology of marine organisms, develop a hypothesis about how body size of these animals may be affected by the zone in which the animal lives. Next, you will test this hypothesis.

1. Using the data from the whole class, calculate the mean, standard deviation, and 95% confidence interval for each of the morphometic measurements taken for the four species at each of the three tidal locations (low, middle, and high tide).
2. Compare these means among the three tidal locations graphically and using the 95% confidence interval method. Do any of the four species display differences in size between tidal zones? Do these results support or refute your hypothesis?

LITERATURE CITED

Ambrose, H. W. A. III., K. P. Ambrose, D. J. Emlen, and K. L. Bright. 2007. *A handbook of biological investigation*. 7th edition. Hunter Textbooks, Inc., Winston Salem, NC. 198 pp.

Bourdeau, P. E., and N. J. O'Connor. 2003. Predation by the nonindigenous Asian shore crab *Hemigrapsus sanguineus* on macroalgae and molluscs. *Northeastern Naturalist* 10:319-334.

Gosner, K. L. 1979. *A field guide to the Atlantic seashore: The Bay of Fundy to Cape Hatteras*. Houghton Mifflin Co., Boston. 329 pp.

Kolar, C. S., and D. M. Lodge. 2001. *Progress in invasion biology: predicting invaders. Trends in Ecology and Evolution* 16:199-204.

Little, C., G. A. Williams, and C. D. Trowbridge. 2009. *The biology of rocky shores*. 2nd edition. Oxford University Press, Oxford. 356 pp.

FIELD WORKSHEET

You should read the Case Study completely before coming to the field site. This worksheet is designed to provide you with a step by step overview of the procedures and protocols that you will be carrying out at the field site.

- Set up your transect on the beach measuring from the high tide line, which is marked by a band of flotsam and jetsam left by the high tide.
- With your metric tape measure from the high tide line **20m, 35m, and 50m** distances.
- Mark each location with a stake that is labeled 20m, 35m or 50m.
- At each of the three sampling distances or sites, place the standardized circular samplers (76.2 centimeter diameter samplers).
- Use a die or other random method to determine which of the four possible quadrats will not be sampled.

UPPER BEACH

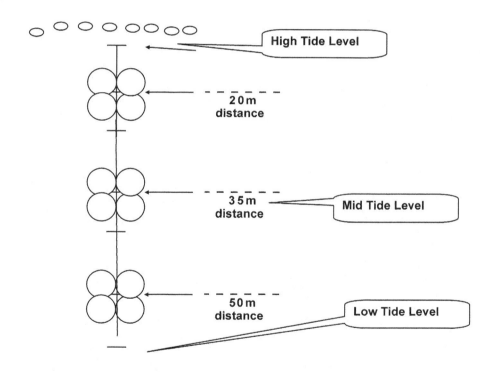

OCEAN

- Place your sampler over each selected sector and count the number of individuals for each species listed on your data sheet.
- Record the species count data for each sample.
- Repeat the procedure at each of the selected sampling distances.
- *Carefully record your data on the data sheet provided. Before leaving today you must record your raw count data on the sheet labeled "Field Report Sheet." Note that this sheet also has a place for you to report the diameter of your sampler. Make sure this sheet is complete and correct and that the diameter of the sampler is reported. One copy of this sheet for each research team MUST be turned in to your lab instructor before you leave the beach study area.*
- **Beach Stewardship:**
Once your Research Team has finished with the data gathering you will be given a bag in which to collect beach debris. This material will be brought back to the campus, sorted and cataloged, and then either recycled or disposed of in a proper manner.

INTERTIDAL ZONATION FIELD TRIP DATA SHEET: RESEARCH TEAM COPY
ECOLOGY LAB

DATA SHEET FOR QUADRAT SAMPLING: RESEARCH TEAM DATA

DATE:_____   Research Team:_____

Team Members:_____

Diameter of Sampler:_____   Area of Sampler:_____

Site and Quadrat Number: Distance from High Tide Edge (meters)	Species 1: Common Periwinkle Count		Species 2: Asian Shore Crab Count		Species 3: Blue Mussel Count		Species 4: Green Crab Count	
Q1-1: Distance (m): 20			2					
Q1-2 (High Tide)								
Q1-3								
Q2-1: Distance (m): 35								
Q2-2 (Mid Tide)								
Q2-3								
Q3-1: Distance (m) 50								
Q3-2 (Low Tide)								
Q3-3								
Total Count at 20 m								

Total Count at 35 m				
Total Count at 50 m				
Avg. Count at 20 m				
Avg. Count at 35 m				
Avg. Count at 50 m				
Standard Dev. 20 m				
Standard Dev. 35 m				
Standard Dev. 50 m				
Variance 20 m				
Variance 35 m				
Variance 50 m				
Organisms/sq M 20 m				
Organisms/sq M 35 m				
Organisms/sq M 50 m				
GPS Reading 20 m				
GPS Reading 35 m				
GPS Reading 50 m				

INTERTIDAL ANIMAL MORPHOMETRICS DATA SHEET: RESEARCH TEAM COPY

DATE:_____
Research Team Number:_____
Team Members:_____

DATA SHEET
Intertidal Animal Morphometics

		Periwinkles	Asian Shore Crab	Green Crab	Blue Mussel
Low Tide	1				
Low Tide	2				
Low Tide	3				
Low Tide	4				
Low Tide	5				
Low Tide	6				
Low Tide	7				
Low Tide	8				
Low Tide	9				
Low Tide	10				
Mean Tide	1				
Mean Tide	2				
Mean Tide	3				
Mean Tide	4				
Mean Tide	5				
Mean Tide	6				
Mean Tide	7				
Mean Tide	8				
Mean Tide	9				
Mean Tide	10				
High Tide	1				
High Tide	2				
High Tide	3				
High Tide	4				
High Tide	5				
High Tide	6				
High Tide	7				
High Tide	8				
High Tide	9				
High Tide	10				

Diameter of Sampler:_____ Area of Sampler:_____

CHAPTER 6 ASSIGNMENT 1 FIELD ASSIGNMENT

At the end of today's field trip this sheet must be turned in to the laboratory instructor.

Research Team number _____ Date: _____
Names: _____

_____

_____

_____

GPS Coordinates of upper beach site   N _____   W _____
GPS Coordinates of middle beach site   N _____   W _____
GPS Coordinates of lower beach site   N _____   W _____

Weather conditions: _____

Air temperature: _____   Wind direction _____   Wind Speed _____

Site and Quadrat Number	Species 1	Species 2	Species 3	Species 4
Distance from High Tide Edge (meters)	Common Periwinkle	Asian Shore Crab	Blue Mussel	Green Crab
	Count	Count	Count	Count
Q1-1: Distance (m): 15				
Q1-2 (High Tide)				
Q1-3				
Q2-1: Distance (m): 30				
Q2-2 (Mid Tide)				
Q2-3				
Q3-1: Distance (m) 45				
Q3-2 (Low Tide)				
Q3-3				

CHAPTER 6 ASSIGNMENT 2 LAB ASSIGNMENT

At the end of today's lab, this sheet must be turned in to the laboratory instructor.

Name: _____

Research Team number _____   Date: _____

Each person in each research team must select one of the four species (Periwinkles, Green Crab, Asian Shore Crab or Blue Mussel). Each team member must select a different species.

For your selected species your assignment is to do a Chi Square Analysis for this species comparing the species distribution at the 20 meter, 35 meter and 50 meter intertidal locations and to make one chart (either a histogram or a pie chart or another variety of chart that is appropriate for count (discrete) data).

Print out the result of your analysis and your charts and attach all the analysis pages and charts to this sheet and turn in to the laboratory instructor before the end of today's laboratory.

Species selected (circle): blue mussel, green crab, Asian shore crab, periwinkle

C H A P T E R 7

Guidelines for Laboratory Reports

Communicating the results of your work is an important aspect of any career in biology. It enables people to learn about your discovery and replicate your methods of investigation, either to confirm your results or apply your approach to solving additional research problems. Scientific writing is quite different from writing in other disciplines, so in this chapter we present a guide to producing written reports for this course. Additional details, suggestions, and examples can be found in McMillan (2006), among other sources.

In this course, we will produce two types of reports. The first is a short report in the format of a letter to a state or local agency. The second is longer and more detailed, in the standard format of articles published in scientific journals. Below, we present guidelines for each type of report.

WRITING LABORATORY REPORTS IN THE FORMAT OF A LETTER REPORT

For three of the case studies your laboratory reports will take the form of a letter. This letter should contain complete information about your study. The letter should be addressed to the Conservation Commission of the Town in which the study took place or other appropriate agency as identified in the Case Study. Memo reports are short and do not require the detailed literature search and information that is required in a scientific paper report. However they must contain the following information.

Where: Where was the study performed? Make sure to include the exact GPS coordinates for the study site, a field sketch of the study site and a Google Earth image showing the study site.

When: When was the study performed, including the date and the time of day?

Data: Present your data. This may be in the form of a table.

Analysis: Present an analysis of your data.

Discussion and Conclusion: A brief discussion of your study and the major findings or results of your study.

Signature and Contact information: You should sign your memo or letter and include contact information including your name, telephone number, mailing address and email address.

Other things that you might include (optional):

Photographs of the study site

Photographs of organism or organisms studied

The following is an example of what a letter report might look like.

John C. Jahoda, Ph.D.
Professor of Biology
Department of Biological Sciences
Bridgewater State University
Bridgewater, MA 02325
Email: jjahoda@bridgew.edu

April 6, 2011

Conservation Commission
Town of Bridgewater
Town Office
Bridgewater, MA 02324

Dear Commissioners:

From Tuesday March 15, 2011 to Saturday March 19, 2011 I conducted a study of the southern flying squirrel, *Glaucomys volans*, in the woodlots surrounding Carver Pond in Bridgewater, MA using remote infrared photography. A total of 20 infrared cameras were set up with remote triggers. The triggers were placed under 8 inch pie plates placed in the trees and baited with non-salted peanuts. When a flying squirrel landed in the plate the weight of the squirrel triggered the camera to take a picture of the squirrel. The camera was set up to place a time and date stamp on each digital photograph so that we could determine the date and time of each photo taken.

Camera traps were placed in four habitat types around the pond: White Pine Woodlot, Red Maple Forest, Beech Grove, and Oak Woodlot.

Five camera traps were placed in each of the four habitat types.

The GPS coordinates for the four habitat types are as follows:
White Pine Woodlot: 41°58′45.64″ N and 70°58′10.44″ W
Red Maple Forest: 41°58′44.89″ N and 70°57′58.31″ W
Beech Grove: 41°58′46.72″ N and 70°57′54.53″ W
Oak Woodlot: 41°58′41.32″ N and 70°57′58.95″ W

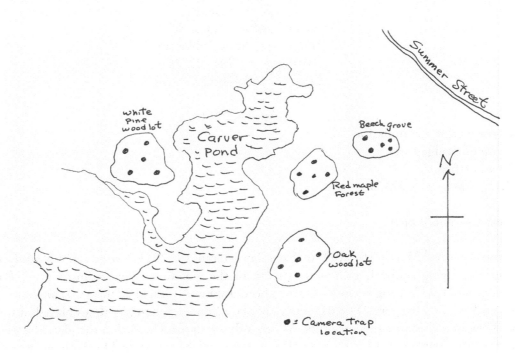

Figure 1. A sketch map of the Carver Pond area showing
the location of the four habitat types with trap locations.

The results of this study were as follows:

Squirrels Photographed

Date	White Pine Woodlot	Red Oak Woodlot	Maple Woodlot	Beach Grove
15-Mar	3	6	3	1
16-Mar	2	8	3	2
17-Mar	1	10	4	1
18-Mar	5	14	2	2
19-Mar	2	17	2	3
Totals	13	55	14	9

Flying squirrel activity was clearly non-random (χ=61.57, DF=3, P<0.001), with flying squirrels showing a preference for the Oak Woodlots in the vicinity of Carver Pond. Therefore, I recommend that flying squirrel conservation activities focus on this habitat type.

Sincerely,

John C. Jahoda, Ph.D.

WRITING LABORATORY REPORTS IN THE FORMAT OF A SCIENTIFIC RESEARCH PAPER

For one of the four case studies (see Chapter 6), you will prepare a laboratory report in the format of a scientific research paper, such as you would find in a professional journal. To complete this task, several steps will be necessary. First, each research team will be responsible for data collection in the field. Thereafter, teams of two students will collaborate to complete data analysis and graphing of results. Each student will then use these results individually to produce a complete research report.

An example of a Scientific Research Paper

Because scientific papers typically contain a great deal of information, much of which can be quite complex and technical, it is critical that they are clear, concise, and follow a standard format. Before you begin working on your papers, we will take some time in the laboratory to analyze and discuss an excellent example of a paper that has all the elements you will need to incorporate into your laboratory reports. The paper that we have chosen for this analysis is:

Quinn, J. S., and J. Sirdevan. 1998. Experimental measurement of nesting substrate preference in Caspian terns, *Sterna caspia*, and the successful colonization of human constructed islands. Biological Conservation 85: 63-68.

A copy of this paper with annotations is posted on the course home page, in the Laboratory Handouts section under Course Documents. This paper will serve as an example of the format and style that you should follow in your laboratory reports. A set of guidelines outlining the requirements for your research report, the suggested format and style, and additional suggestions are presented below.

General Format of Your Paper

Your paper must be written with the use of a word processor having a 12 pt. font. We recommend using Microsoft Word, which is available on the university network, although other file types that are compatible with Word are acceptable. It is important that your report be complete, organized, well written, and concise. In the biological sciences, the general format for writing a scientific paper includes the following sections:

    Title page
    Introduction
    Materials and Methods
    Results
    Discussion
    Acknowledgments
    Literature Cited 2 primarys, 4 total

Optional Sections may include:
    Abstract
    Summary
    Conclusions last phragraph of discussion.

Placement of Figures and Tables:

Tables and figures should be numbered sequentially (e.g., Table 1, Table 2, etc.), and they should appear near where they are first mentioned in the text. Particularly in older papers, you might find all figures and tables placed as appendices at the end of the paper. This approach is now obsolete, as modern word processors easily accommodate tables and figures inserted directly into the text. A paper with the tables and figures presented as they are encountered is easier to read because the reader does not need to flip back and forth repeatedly between the body of the paper and the appendix.

Refer to the suggestions outlined by McMillan (2006) for writing papers in the biological sciences and Ambrose et al. (2007) for methods of data analysis and presentation of figures and tables of data. The style manual of McMillan (2006) will be the final authority on matters of format and style for these papers.

Revision:

We suggest that you discuss your topic and any problems you are having locating sources with your instructor. Your laboratory instructor will review and grade the paper and return it to you for revision. At this point you can either accept the grade given, or you can revise the paper following the suggestions given and resubmit it for an improved grade. Comments will be upon style, format, sources, proper reference citation, presentation of tables and figures, and other aspects of the paper.

Use of Software to prepare your Report:

Word processing has mostly replaced typewriters. You should use a personal computer in the preparation of your report. We recommend the use of Microsoft Word, which is featured on the university computer system, but other software packages (e.g., WordPerfect, Open Office) are also acceptable. Be sure to make use of helpful features such as "spell check," the thesaurus, and functions for export or import of text. However, we urge caution regarding the use of spell checks. There are some perfectly good words in the English language that spell check may recognize but that are not the word you want. In addition, if you are not observant, spell check might replace a misspelled word with a word you don't want. Worse, most built-in dictionaries in word processing programs lack entries for many commonly used scientific terms. Consequently, your word processor might encourage you to change the spelling of a term even if you've spelled it correctly.

The moral of this story is that there is no substitute for careful proofreading. Use spell check with caution, and carefully read over the paper to make sure that any changes make sense.

To complete a research report, you will need to produce tables and figures to display your results. Several software packages are available that can be used to create bar and line graphs. Some examples include DeltaGraph, KaleidaGraph, and SigmaPlot. Microsoft Excel also has extensive graphing capabilities, and figures produced in Excel can be easily imported into a Word document.

Starting Your Reports:

You can do a great deal of the preparatory work for your report early by completing the following items before you have finished your data collection and analysis.
1. Complete your literature search.
2. Write a draft copy of the Introduction and Materials and Methods sections.
3. Choose the statistics you plan to use to analyze your data. Consult Ambrose et al (2007) for examples.

Once you have completed your data collection, complete your analysis, develop graphs and tables, and write your Results and Discussion sections. Many scientific calculators have simple statistical functions that you can use. Microsoft Excel has statistical analysis capabilities as part of some of the special functions in the spreadsheet. Consult the manual on how to load these or ask the computer lab coordinator.

Overview of Each Section:

The required paper in the course should take the form of a research paper in the biological sciences as discussed by McMillan (2006). As such it should include the following sections:

TITLE: The title will be the source of keywords that may be used to find the paper using search engines. Thus, the title should briefly describe your project using words that are relevant to the study.

ABSTRACT: The abstract is a brief overview of your paper. It provides the reader with enough information to decide whether or not to read the paper. Thus the abstract needs to briefly discuss what you did, why you did it, how you did it, and what you found out. The abstract should be no more than a paragraph in length. This section is an optional section. You may include it if you wish, as many journals do include this section, but you are not required to have an abstract.

INTRODUCTION: This should be a brief introduction to your topic. What are you going to discuss? What are your major objectives? What is the hypothesis you chose to investigate? What is the existing state of knowledge about your topic based on the published literature? A good Introduction will inform readers of the major research questions/hypotheses that will be addressed in the paper. Equally importantly, though, it will clearly state WHY it is important to answer those questions. After you write your Introduction, apply the "why should we care" test: if your Introduction doesn't make it clear why your topic is important, then it needs more work. References to background information from journals, books, or previous reports should follow the Harvard Scientific Citation method discussed in McMillan (2006).

MATERIALS AND METHODS: Present answers to all the basic questions about the study: When, Where and How. Maps or diagrams should be given a figure number and legend. Refer to the figure number in your description of your study area or methods. Show locations of your sampling sites on maps of your field study. Give the time period of your study (year, month, day, and time) when it is relevant. Note any relationship to season, time of day, or other natural cycles that influenced the timing of your study.

Explain techniques used to collect and analyze data. Identify equipment you use by the manufacturer, model number or other descriptive information that identifies the specific item used. If you manufactured the equipment yourself, describe it in detail and consider including a diagram. If a sampling method or statistical analysis is a standard method, then you can refer to a literature citation that discuses the method rather than repeat the details of the procedure. Be sure to refer to any computer programs you use to analyze your data.

This section must provide enough information that someone else could follow the same procedures and replicate your study.

RESULTS: This section is a summary of the data and a presentation of the results of statistical analyses. Do not simply present raw data. Instead, write about the trends or patterns you observed in your data, and use Tables or Figures to help readers visualize your results. Summarize data by using descriptive statistics such as the mean and standard deviation, and include appropriate test statistics (e.g., Chi-square), when you report the results of analyses.

Use tables and figures such as graphs and charts to display your data in ways that most effectively show the reader any important trends. Remember that each figure or table should be there for the purpose of making a point with the reader. It should promote understanding of the results. If a particular result can be described easily in one or two sentences, a table or figure is probably unnecessary to illustrate it.

For additional details on presenting results, consult Ambrose et al. (2007). Remember that the Results section should be free of any interpretation of the data. Interpretation is the key part of the Discussion section.

DISCUSSION: Here you should interpret your results in detail. There are several questions that you can ask yourself as you prepare to write this section. For example, what were the major findings and conclusions of other investigators doing similar work? How do the works of different investigators compare to one another? How do your findings compare to these other studies? What are your thoughts on the subject? What conclusions can you draw about your initial hypotheses? Are there any potential sources or error or inadequacies in techniques that might have affected your conclusions? What suggestions do you have for future research on this topic? Make sure you support any points you wish to make with solid logic and literature citations. The majority of your literature citations should occur in this section.

SUMMARY: This section is a brief summation of your research. Usually summaries are in the form of an outline or list which lists the major points made in the paper. This is an optional section and few journals require a summary.

CONCLUSIONS: Most journals include the conclusions as the last paragraph or paragraphs of the discussion section. However, there are some journals which require that the major conclusions be included in a separate section near the very end of the text portion of the paper, just before the acknowledgements. You may separate your conclusions into a conclusion section if you wish. If you do not include a conclusions section, your conclusions must be stated at the end of your discussion.

LITERATURE CITED: This is a list of the journals, books, and papers you actually cited in the text, tables, and figures of your paper. These are listed alphabetically by the last name of the primary author of each reference. The format used here is outlined in McMillan (2006). Consult this resource for detailed examples of the application of these guidelines.

Conducting a Literature Search for your Paper

Your paper should present background and support information from both PRIMARY and SECONDARY literature. Primary literature is a journal article on the original research finding of the author(s) investigating a particular subject. The LITERATURE CITED section of these papers can serve as a means of finding additional papers that may be of interest. Secondary literature includes books, review articles, and textbooks. These do not report the author's original research work but attempt to summarize the knowledge in the field. See the chapter in McMillan (2006) on searching the literature for tips on resources, note taking, and organization.

Your major research report must include a MINIMUM OF FOUR REFERENCES. Two of these references must be primary sources. You may include more than two primary sources, and you may also include any number of secondary references. PRIMARY literature as noted above is a PEER REVIEWED journal article reporting on the original research findings of the author(s). Anything else is secondary. Field Guides, Textbooks, Lab Handouts, etc. are all secondary. Internet resources may also be included. However, only certain internet resources will qualify as PRIMARY. To be primary, an internet resource must meet the requirement of being a report of original research and must be peer reviewed. The majority of these will be on-line versions of a print journal. Thus, a journal article that appeared in a peer-reviewed print journal and is also available on the internet would qualify as a PRIMARY source. Something on a fish and game department webpage, although useful, would not qualify as primary and would be considered a secondary resource. If you have any questions about a particular reference, ask your instructor. In some cases you may be able to use abstracts only and may not require the entire article. If the abstract provides enough information you might not need to acquire the full article. If you use an abstract only you should note after the citation, "(abstract only)."

For certain topics, especially those dealing with local environmental issues, the traditional sources (journals, books, etc.) may not be especially helpful. Information may be found in alternative sources such as Field Reports from State or Federal Agencies, Planning Reports, Governmental documents, Consultant's reports, Town Records, Publications of Environmental Groups and Personal Contacts (Personal Communications) with the people involved. This is perfectly acceptable. Information gathered in this way should also be properly cited in the text. In these cases, the distinction between a primary source and a secondary source may be less clear. In general, if the paper reports direct findings of research made by the writer, it is a primary source. If it presents the findings of others, it is a secondary source.

Where to Locate References:

There are several literature guides, abstracts, and computerized CD-ROM literature search services available in the University Library. Some of the CD-ROM services which may be available include *Biological Abstracts, General Science Abstracts, and Applied Science and Technology.*

In the biological sciences the most useful abstract is *Biological Abstracts*. Bound volumes of old issues are located in the library. Literature is cataloged in several useful ways including subject, author, and key words. Consult with one of the reference librarians if it is your first time using an abstract. McMillan (2006) has a brief discussion of how to conduct a search using *Biological Abstracts*. Check with the reference librarian to determine it the library carries the sources that you need. If the journal is not available in the library, it can usually be obtained for you through a cooperative arrangement with other local college and university libraries or through inter-library loan. Ask the librarians for help with either library cooperative loans or inter-library loans, but <u>allow several weeks to obtain the sources.</u>

Another effective way of finding references is to use internet search engines such as Google Scholar, AltaVista etc. In addition, many print journals now have online versions or have their table of contents available on line. Some journals, in fact (e.g., those published by the Public Library of Science, PloS), are available only online.

The Use of the Internet to Locate Resources:

Google has several search options, including Google Scholar, which gets more research-oriented papers, and Google images, which will get pictures suitable for use in PowerPoint. Image credit should be given for all images used in your presentations.

There are pros and cons in the use of the Internet. The major advantage of the Internet is that Internet sources may be much more up-to-date than books or even journals. The major problem with the Internet is that most of the material posted is not peer-reviewed. This means that there is no guarantee that the information is accurate. There are Internet postings in which the data presented and the arguments made are entirely fictitious. There is no absolute way to avoid this problem, but there are some general guidelines that can help. First, many print journals also publish on the internet. These sources are as safe as the print journal itself, and are considered to be primary sources. Sources such as web pages of major research organizations, universities, colleges, and museums are also probably safe sources, as are those of federal or state agencies. Sources to be avoided are personal web pages or blogs or web pages of unknown or suspect organizations such as the "creation research institute." Materials posted in such places often represent personal opinions and have little or no real data to back them up. When researching a topic using the Internet it is critical to consider the credibility of your sources.

Use of Harvard Scientific Method of Citation within the text:

Each reference that appears in the Literature Cited must also be cited in the text. The system of citation used in science is not the same as that used in English, history, and other fields in the humanities. Citation in science typically does not use a system of footnotes, as is common in these other fields. Instead, the author's name(s) and the year of publication are inserted into a sentence to identify the source of information. For example:

The intensity of competition may diminish if the abundance of superior competitors is reduced by predation (Paine, 1966) or disturbance (Connell, 1978).

Rosenzweig (1992, 1995) suggested that latitudinal gradients in species richness result chiefly from increased land area in the tropics.

Desiccation, especially of eggs and young individuals, is a primary cause of snail mortality (Heatwole and Heatwole, 1978; Riddle, 1983; Solem, 1984; Baur and Baur, 1993).

Note that when the author is referred to by name in the sentence, the date is given in parentheses after his or her name. Also note that if several papers by the same author are being referenced, the dates are listed in order and separated by a comma. When several different papers are referenced, they are cited in the order they appear in the Literature Cited section and separated by semi-colons. When a paper has three or more authors, it is cited using the first author's name only and the abbreviation "et al." (e.g., Smith et al., 1959). The abbreviation, "et al.," is for the Latin phrase meaning "and others." Look at several papers in biological journals and see how the citations are made in the text. Consult McMillan (2006) for other specific examples of citations, including types of references that we did not discuss in detail here, such as symposia and personal communications.

Quotations:

Do not use extensive quotations. Quotations should only be used if the exact wording is the focus of discussion or if the wording in the original source is so good that it cannot be easily paraphrased. Instead, re-state the idea in your own words and cite the original source.

Alternative methods of Citation for Ecology Papers:

A number of journals use alternative citation systems instead of the Harvard Scientific Method of Citation (Author/Date) system. Although we recognize the validity of these alternatives, in this course we will, for the sake of consistency, use only the Harvard Scientific Method of Citation as found in McMillan (2006).

Plagiarism:

Remember that using the unacknowledged exact wording of others is plagiarism. It is illegal and violates copyright law. Plagiarism in your reports is academically dishonest and carries severe penalties. Any report in which plagiarism is detected will receive a grade of zero. Some students attempt to avoid plagiarism by copying sentences from their sources but changing a few words. This is NOT a solution. You should take the information from your literature resources and re-state it in your own words. Even then, you must properly attribute the information (i.e., always cite the source of any factual information and any ideas that you did not develop yourself).

Tables and Figures:

Use Microsoft Excel, Quattro Pro, Harvard Graphics, or some other computerized graphics package to develop and print your tables and figures of data. With the newer word processing programs, these can be included within the text where they are first encountered or referenced. Be sure to make them large enough so that they can be easily read and comprehended by the reader. See McMillan (2006) for a complete discussion of how to construct tables and figures. Below are some key points for you to remember:
  • Tables and Figures are sequentially numbered with Arabic numerals in the order that they are first mentioned in the text of your paper.

- Explanatory legends are placed above tables and underneath figures.
- The axes of the figure (if it is a graphical presentation) should be clearly specified and the units and scale identified.
- Legends for both figures and tables must give enough information so that they can be understood without referring to the next.
- Leave adequate margins on pages with tables and figures. Use the same margins that are used in the text.
- Refer to all tables and figures by parenthetical citations, e.g. (Table 1), or (Figure 3), at the appropriate point in the text.

Other Considerations:

All pages should be numbered starting with the second page. The first page or title page is not numbered. This page should include only the title of your paper, the course name and number, and your name. The text of the paper starts on the second page.

All scientific names must be *italicized*. All modern word processing programs allow you to italicize words. If italics are not available (e.g., most type writers), underline scientific names. See McMillan (2006) for other specifics on style and format.

LITERATURE CITED

Ambrose, H. W. A. III., K. P. Ambrose, D. J. Emlen, and K. L. Bright. 2007. *A handbook of biological investigation.* 7th edition. Hunter Textbooks, Inc., Winston Salem, N.C. 198 pp.

Council of Biology Editors, Committee on Form and Style. 1978. *CBE style manual.* 4th edition. American Institute of Biological Sciences, Washington, D.C.

McMillan, V. E. 2006. *Writing papers in the biological sciences.* 4th edition. Bedford/St. Martin's Press, New York. 288 pp.

OTHER USEFUL REFERENCES

Alley, M. 1996. *The craft of scientific writing.* 3rd edition. Springer-Verlag, New York.

Briscoe, M. H. 1996. *Preparing scientific illustrations.* 2nd edition. Springer-Verlag, New York.

Day, R. 1998. *How to write and publish a scientific paper.* 5th edition. Oryx Press, Phoenix, AZ.

Gopen, G. D., and J. A. Swan. 1990. The science of scientific writing. *American Scientist* 78:550-558.

Huth, E. J. 1994. *Scientific style and format: the CBE manual for authors, editors, and publishers.* 6th edition. Cambridge University Press, New York.

Mack, R. N. 1986. Writing with precision, clarity, and economy. *Bulletin of the Ecological Society of America* 67:31-35.

C H A P T E R 8

The Woodlot Project:
A Field Study of Tree Competition

OBJECTIVES

Determine whether white pines compete intensely with each other or with other tree species in a mixed-species woodlot.

INTRODUCTION

One of the major themes in modern ecology is the interaction between individuals or species. A variety of types of interactions can occur, and an individual (or species) can benefit or be harmed by an interaction (or, in some cases, not be affected). Among the negative interactions is competition. Competition takes place when multiple organisms use a resource that is in limited supply (Tilman 1982). Such an interaction always has a negative effect on both participants; for each, the per capita growth rate is depressed and the per capita death rate increased by the presence of the competitor. Over time, this could result in resource partitioning or character displacement, which would reduce or eliminate the negative effects of competition. In this field study, we will be looking for evidence of competition in a forest ecosystem.

COMPETITION AMONG TREES

You are working for a forest management and consulting firm that has received a contract from a local timber holding company to evaluate the effect of tree competition within mixed softwood and hardwood lots in the region. As the first stage in a long-term study to develop a plan for best management strategies for these forests, we need to understand how trees compete with each other for environmental resources. This includes competition between trees of the same species (*intraspecific*) and with trees of other species (*interspecific*).

In applied forest ecology, foresters use a wide range of methods to study the effects of competition so land managers can make decisions that will help achieve ecological goals while providing economically viable yields (Canham et al., 2004). Forest management today often uses predictive models and knowledge of the impacts of competition on forest growth and development.

If trees are competing for resources such as light, water and nutrients, the effect of this competition will be seen in the growth rate of the trees and in the distribution patterns of the trees. One noticeable impact of competition is called "self-thinning" (Westoby 1984). In a stand of trees, as individuals age and grow, some of the trees in the stand will die as a result of competition for resources. Thus, older stands will be made up of fewer and larger trees. We can look for this pattern and use it as an indication of competition.

Competition between trees for light, water, or nutrients may influence survivorship and growth in several measurable ways. Mortality of individuals that grow too close to an established, mature tree may lead to uniformity in the spacing of individual trees. Individuals that grow close together may also experience intense competition, which may result in some stunting of growth.

ALLOMETRICS AND SIZE OF TREES

Allometry is the study of the relative growth rates, or the change in proportion of various parts of an organism as a consequence of growth. It can also be defined as the phenomenon whereby parts of the same organism grow at different rates. If you know the allometrics of a particular species you can use one measurement to determine other measurements. In the study of trees, measurement of the size of the tree is very often important. An allometric measurement that is widely used in forestry and dendrology is known as Diameter at Breast Height (DBH). This is the diameter of the tree taken at 1.37 m (4.5 feet) above the forest floor on the uphill side of a tree. DBH is a traditional forestry measurement and is used in many allometry calculations to determine things like growth, volume, yield and forest potential. DBH is the most frequent measurement made by a forester. The DBH is taken using a diameter tape or tree caliper.

Instead of the DBH, we will use a different allometric for this study, the Circumference at Breast Height (CBH), which is an easier measurement to take. Because there is a constant ratio between DBH and CBH as shown by the following formula, this will not affect our analyses.

Circumference at Breast Height = Pi times Diameter at Breast Height

$$CBH = \pi\, DBH$$

Or

Diameter at Breast Height = Circumference at Breast Height divided by Pi

$$DBH = CBH / \pi$$

In these equations, π (the Greek letter pi) is defined as the ratio of the circumference of the circle to its diameter (the numerical value of pi is approximately 3.1415927).

OUR STUDY

Our preliminary study will be an investigation of a stand of mixed forest that contains maple, *Acer spp*, white pine, *Pinus strobus,* and oak, *Quercus spp.* The oaks include several species, including white oak *Quercus alba*, red oak, *Quercus rubra*, and black oak, *Quercus velutina.* The majority of the maples are red maple, *Acer rubrum.* Within the study area, each research team will select 30 white pines for study. These pines will be referred to as *focal trees.*

Figure 8-1. Mixed species stand of white pines and hardwood species suitable
for the study of tree competition.

FIELD METHODS

Differences in topography, moisture conditions, or substrate type will impose variations on the
growth of trees that are the same distance apart. These variations will make the detection of
competitive influences very difficult, even though such influences may be important. Thus,
you should control for these effects by selecting a relatively flat area without any major variation in exposure, topography, substrate, or moisture conditions.

In this preliminary study, we will focus on the white pine. Each research team will select thirty (30) white pines as focal trees.

Randomly select 30 white pine trees as your focal trees. In selecting your trees try to cover the
entire size range from small trees to large trees so that you have at least some small pine trees,
medium-sized pine trees and large pine trees in your sample. Make sure your focal trees are
far enough away from the focal trees selected by other research teams to prevent any focal trees
from being counted as nearest neighbor trees. All focal trees should be marked with the colored flagging provided to your research team so that you can assure that no focal trees are close
enough to be a nearest neighbor tree. All focal trees must be over 10 cm CBH to avoid using
saplings as focal trees. Nearest neighbor trees can be of any size.

Nearest Neighbor method
The method we will use to look at competition is to measure the distance between the focal
tree and its "nearest neighbor" and measure the size of the focal tree and the nearest neighbor.
We will then to do a correlation analysis on the data set. For each focal tree you will need to
collect several measurements, summarized below.

1. For each focal tree, measure the Circumference at Breast Height (CBH). Then measure the distance from this tree to the nearest neighbor (i.e., the closest individual) of the same species (Pine to Pine). Use this distance as a radius of a circle around your focal tree and be sure it does not overlap the focal tree of another research team. Measure the CBH of the nearest neighbor. These data will be combined for all the research teams in your laboratory section and analyzed for evidence of intraspecific competition.

2. Now measure the distance from the focal tree to the nearest neighbor of a different species (Pine to Maple, Pine to Oak, etc.). Measure the CBH of the nearest neighbor. These data will be combined for all research teams in your laboratory section and analyzed for evidence of **interspecific** competition.

Figure 8-2. Measuring the circumference of the focal tree.

Selection of focal trees: As noted above you will sample a total of 30 focal trees. Select your focal trees randomly but be sure to try to cover the entire size range of large, medium and small trees in your sample of 30 white pine trees. All focal trees must be larger than 10 cm CBH.

When you select your focal tree, mark it with colored flagging. The other research teams in the laboratory section will do the same. Do not use a focal tree that has been used previously by either your research team or another research team in the laboratory section and make sure your focal tree is far enough away from other focal trees to avoid using any team's focal tree as a neighbor tree.

Marking of trees: The flagging should be left on all the focal trees while data is being gathered. This will prevent a tree from being sampled more than once. At the end of the laboratory section, when all teams have selected and measured all their focal trees and all data has been collected, remove all the flagging from the trees.

Data must be recorded on the data forms for all focal trees. Make sure your data form is complete and you have not only recorded your research team's data, but have exchanged data with the other research teams in your laboratory section and have a complete set of data before leaving the field site.

ANALYTICAL METHODS

Correlation analysis (see Chapter 9) will be used to test for a relationship between the CBH of the two "neighbors," as well as to test for a relationship between CBH of a tree and the distance to its nearest neighbor. A strong positive correlation between these two values (size and distance) is seen as a strong indication of competition.

The analysis you will do using the Pearson's correlation coefficient will involve setting up the data and then running the program to obtain the correlation coefficient. This analysis should be run for the following pairings.

CBH of focal tree vs. CBH of Nearest Neighbor of the same species
CBH of focal tree vs. Distance to Nearest Neighbor of same species
CBH of focal tree vs. CBH of Nearest Neighbor of the other species
CBH of focal tree vs. Distance to Nearest Neighbor of other species

For this analysis, you will use the data from all the research teams in your laboratory section. The data form has space for you to gather and exchange data from the other research teams in your laboratory section. This should be done before you leave the field site.

Figure 8-3. The circumference of the tree is measured at breast height.

Figure 8-4. Measuring the circumference of a large pine for CBH determination.

Data Analysis (Nearest Neighbor Method)

This analysis can be done on the combined data from all the research teams from your laboratory section. Each research team will only have data on 30 trees. The data set can be strengthened by including the data from the other research teams in your lab section in the analysis.

For each data set, the first thing you will need to do is input the data from your laboratory section into the Excel analysis sheet, which is posted on the course website. The sheet is already set up to use CBH (circumference breast height) as measured in the field.

You will need to copy and then use the commands edit / paste special / values in Excel on the entire data set before proceeding, this will allow you to avoid doing recalculations when you copy and paste data. Once you have done this, use the copy and paste commands to create a series of four data sets, one for each of the following comparisons:

1. CBH of focal tree vs. CBH of nearest neighbor of the same species
2. CBH of focal tree vs. CBH of nearest neighbor of another species
3. CBH of focal tree vs. distance to the nearest neighbor of the same species
4. CBH of focal tree vs. distance to the nearest neighbor of another species

For each data set, use the Excel Chart Wizard to produce a graph of the data. Use the scatterplot so your X and Y values are correlated on your graph.

For each data set calculate a correlation coefficient. To do this, choose an empty cell near the data set and use the CORREL function: "=CORREL ([Data])". Instead of typing in the data, you will simply select all of the cells on your worksheet that contain data for the test. This will only work if your two variables are in adjacent columns. The CORREL function will return a correlation coefficient (r). Compare this value to the appropriate critical value of correlation coefficients based on the total number of trees measured in your lab section (Table

8-1). Use this number to test the null hypothesis that there is no correlation between variables. Interpret these results as directed in Chapter 9.

Table 8-1: Selected critical values for Pearson's correlation coefficient (r) for $\alpha = 0.05$ (calculated using Lowry 2011).

Sample Size (n)	Critical Correlation Coefficient (r)
30	0.361
60	0.254
90	0.207
120	0.180
150	0.161
210	0.136

If competition is pervasive at the study site, we should observe a positive correlation between the CBH of the focal tree and the distance to the nearest neighbor. Also, there should be a positive correlation between the CBH of the focal tree and the CBH of the nearest neighbor. Both of these results should occur because small individuals growing near a large neighbor should be at a competitive disadvantage, and are likely to die before reaching adulthood. The strength of the correlation should be indicative of the intensity of competition. If the competition is weak, the correlation coefficient may be small (close to zero). If the competition is strong, the correlation coefficient may be large (close to one).

KEY TO FOCAL TREE SPECIES

a. Leaves broad and flat, scattered along the twigs. No cones produced, Leaves with veins radiating from base of blade ... Go to 2

b. Leaves needle-like, clustered in 5's on the twigs. Cones present ....*Pinus strobus*

a. Fruits flat with two wings, Bark smooth and grayish ....*Acer rubrum*

b. Fruits nut (Acorn), Bark rough and corrugated..*Quercus spp*

REPORTING RESULTS

You should report your results in the format of a Research Memo (letter) to the local Conservation Commission. Your answers to the questions below and the graphs that you construct should help you to do so. Additional instructions for the production of a good letter report can be found in Chapter 7.

Your analysis will be done using the pooled data for your laboratory section. The number of trees will be 30 if you only have one research team, 60 trees if you have two research teams, 90 trees if you have three research teams and 120 trees if you have four research teams in your laboratory section. Most data sets will be either 90 or 120 trees.

1. Obtain the data from the other research teams in your laboratory section and use this larger data set for all the trees sampled in your laboratory section to conduct the analysis.

2. Use Excel to make a table listing each of the white pine trees in your laboratory section's data set along with the CBH of the pine tree, the CBH of the nearest other pine tree, the CBH of the nearest tree of another species (maple, oak etc.) and the distances between the focal pine tree and these two other trees.

3. Create an XY scatterplot using Excel that compares the CBHs of the focal pine trees, the CBHs of the nearest neighbor of another species, the distance between the focal tree and the nearest other pine tree and the distance between the focal tree and the nearest tree of another species.

4. Calculate the correlation coefficients and construct a table showing the correlation coefficients for each of the relationships using the sample of pine trees in your laboratory section data set.

5. Describe the relationships your data set shows between the pine trees.

6. Describe the relationships your data set shows between the pine trees and the trees of other species (maples, oaks etc.) in the woodlot.

7. Is there any evidence of competition? Where is competition strongest?

8. Is there any evidence of dominance? Which species appears to be dominant in this woodlot?

LITERATURE CITED

Canham, C. D., LePage, P. T., and Coates, K. D. 2004. A neighborhood analysis of canopy tree competition: effects of shading versus crowding. *Canadian Journal of Forest Research* 34:778–787.

Lowry, R. 2011. Calculators for statistical table entries [Internet]. Retrieved April 21, 2011, from http://faculty.vassar.edu/lowry/tabs.html#r

Tilman, D. 1982. *Resource competition and community structure*. Princeton, NJ: Princeton University Press. 296 pp.

Westoby, M. 1984. The self-thinning rule. *Advances in Ecological Research* 14:167-225.

FIELD WORKSHEET

You should read the Case Study completely before coming to the field site. This worksheet is designed to provide you with a step by step overview of the procedures and protocols that you will be carrying out at the field site.

- Select thirty white pines (focal trees). These pines should be of different sizes from small to large.
- Each research team will gather data on a total of thirty focal trees. Mark trees with flagging so they are not included in the study multiple times.
- For each focal tree you will need to collect five pieces of data:

  1. Circumference at breast height of the focal tree (in cm)

  2. Circumference at breast height of the nearest neighbor of the same species (in cm)

  3. Distance (in cm) to nearest neighbor of the same species

  4. Circumference at breast height of the nearest neighbor of another species (in cm)

  5. Distance (in cm) to nearest neighbor of another species.

Data should be recorded on the data forms for all focal trees. You should record the data from your research team on the form and before you leave the field you should exchange data with all the other research teams in your laboratory section so that you have a complete set of data.

TREE COMPETITION
NEAREST NEIGHBOR DATA
PAGE 1

Research Team Number: _____

Research Team Members: _____

Date: _____ Time: _____

Weather conditions: _____

GPS of Research Site.   N _____ W _____

Data from your research team

Focal Tree Number	Focal Tree Circumference (in cm)	SAME SPECIES Intraspecific Circumference (in cm)	SAME SPECIES Intraspecific Distance to (in cm)	OTHER SPECIES Interspecific Circumference (in cm)	OTHER SPECIES Interspecific Distance to (in cm)
1					
2					
3					
4					
5					
6					
7					
8					
9					

10					
11					
12					
13					
14					
15					
16					
17					
18					
19					
20					
21					
22					
23					
24					
25					
26					
27					
28					
29					
30					

TREE COMPETITION
NEAREST NEIGHBOR DATA
PAGE 2

Research Team Number: _____

Research Team Members: _____

Data from other research team 1

Focal Tree Number	Focal Tree Circumference (in cm)	SAME SPECIES Intraspecific Circumference (in cm)	SAME SPECIES Intraspecific Distance to (in cm)	OTHER SPECIES Interspecific Circumference (in cm)	OTHER SPECIES Interspecific Distance to (in cm)
1					
2					
3					
4					
5					
6					
7					
8					
9					

10					
11					
12					
13					
14					
15					
16					
17					
18					
19					
20					
21					
22					
23					
24					
25					
26					
27					
28					
29					
30					

TREE COMPETITION
NEAREST NEIGHBOR DATA
PAGE 3

Research Team Number: __3d__

Research Team Members: __Jessica, Nicole, Steven__

Data from other research team 2

Focal Tree Number	Focal Tree Circumference (in cm)	SAME SPECIES Intraspecific Circumference (in cm)	SAME SPECIES Intraspecific Distance to (in cm)	OTHER SPECIES Interspecific Circumference (in cm)	OTHER SPECIES Interspecific Distance to (in cm)
1	108	26.6	50.6	45.3	16.1
2	54.3	121.6	22.2	19	47.1
3	145.9	66.7	640	515	85
4	152.9	710	165.3	56.5	80
5	165	71.0	150	200	41
6	60	555	84	48	310
7	84.5	75.7	83	30.6	94
8	32	75.7	312	52.5	34
9	84	75.7	50	25.2	123

10					
11					
12					
13					
14					
15					
16					
17					
18					
19					
20					
21					
22					
23					
24					
25					
26					
27					
28					
29					
30					

TREE COMPETITION
NEAREST NEIGHBOR DATA
PAGE 4

Research Team Number: _____

Research Team Members: _____

Data from other research team 3

Focal Tree Number	Focal Tree Circumference (in cm)	SAME SPECIES Intraspecific Circumference (in cm)	SAME SPECIES Intraspecific Distance to (in cm)	OTHER SPECIES Interspecific Circumference (in cm)	OTHER SPECIES Interspecific Distance to (in cm)
1					
2					
3					
4					
5					
6					
7					
8					
9					

10					
11					
12					
13					
14					
15					
16					
17					
18					
19					
20					
21					
22					
23					
24					
25					
26					
27					
28					
29					
30					

Before leaving the field today make sure you have exchanged data with all the other research teams in your laboratory section and that this data form is complete. You will need the complete data set to complete this research project and write your letter report.

CHAPTER 8 ASSIGNMENT 1 FIELD ASSIGNMENT

At the end of today's field trip this sheet must be turned in to the laboratory instructor.

Names: _____

_____

_____

_____

Research Team number _____   Date: _____

GPS Coordinates of research site: N _____ W _____
Weather conditions: _____
Air temperature: _____ Wind direction _____ Wind Speed _____

Focal Tree Number	Focal Tree Circumference (in cm)	SAME SPECIES Intraspecific Circumference (in cm)	SAME SPECIES Intraspecific Distance to (in cm)	OTHER SPECIES Interspecific Circumference (in cm)	OTHER SPECIES Interspecific Distance to (in cm)
1					
2					
3					
4					
5					
6					
7					
8					
9					

10					
11					
12					
13					
14					
15					
16					
17					
18					
19					
20					
21					
22					
23					
24					
25					
26					
27					
28					
29					
30					

All distances and circumferences are measured in centimeters (cm)

CHAPTER 8
ASSIGNMENT 2 LAB ASSIGNMENT

At the end of today's lab, this sheet must be turned in to the laboratory instructor.

Name: _____

Research Team number: _____   Date: _____

1. Using the pooled nearest neighbor data, perform a correlation analysis using Excel.
2. Using the chart wizard function in Excel, plot the outcome of the analysis performed in 1 using a scatter plot.

Attach the results of your analysis to this sheet and turn it in at the end of today's laboratory.

Additional Considerations on Statistics and Data

A conceptual overview of the use of statistics in ecological field studies appears in Chapter 2. If you have not yet read Chapter 2, **read it before proceeding**! This chapter is not meant to duplicate that information. Rather, it is designed to serve as a reference, providing additional details and step-by-step instructions for the analytical techniques you will use to explore your data. The first section of the chapter will discuss descriptive statistics, and the second section will outline the procedure for conducting hypothesis tests used in the case studies.

DESCRIPTIVE STATISTICS

Two types of descriptive statistics that are important in this course are measures of *central tendency* and measures of *variation*. Each will be addressed below.

Measures of Central Tendency

This type of statistic describes the center of a distribution of data points. In other words, it tells us what the "average" value is for a particular characteristic. Even something this simple, though, can be measured in multiple ways (see Fig. 9-1).

- **Mean:** This is the most commonly used measure of central tendency. When most people say the word "average," they're referring to the mean. It is calculated as the sum of all observations divided by the number of observations (n).

$$\overline{x} = \frac{(\Sigma \, x_i)}{n}$$

  The mean can be calculated easily in Excel, using the AVERAGE function (see Chapter 2).

- **Median:** If you were to arrange all of your data points in order from greatest to least, then the median would be the value in the center (i.e., there are equally many values above and below it). If there is an even number of data points, the median would be the mean of the middle two values. The median is most useful if there are extreme values in the data set that might inflate the mean. In Excel, you can use the MEDIAN function to identify the median for a set of numbers.

- **Mode:** This is the value that occurs most frequently in the data set. Note that there could be multiple modes (or no mode at all) in a particular data set. In Excel, the function MODE will find the modal value for a set of numbers.

Value	Mean:
2	
2	$\bar{x} = \dfrac{(\Sigma\, x_i)}{n} = \dfrac{(2 + 2 + 2 + 3 + 5 + 6 + 9)}{7} = 4.14$
2	
3	Median:
5	The "middle" value is 3.
6	
9	Mode:
	The most common value is 2.

Fig. 9-1: A comparison of measures of central tendency. Notice that, for a single data set, the three measures can be very different.

Measures of Variation

This type of descriptive statistic tells us how much variability there is among individuals within a sample, or how much variability there is among samples. This is important in hypothesis testing because we cannot identify a significant difference between two samples unless we know how precise our estimates are. There are many possible measures of variation, but we will focus on two.

- **Standard deviation:** This statistic measures how individual data points are distributed around a mean. It can be calculated as:

$$S = \sqrt{\frac{\Sigma(x_i - \bar{x})^2}{(n-1)}}$$

  The mean is subtracted from each data point (x_i), and then these differences are squared and added together (as indicated by "Σ"). This total is divided by one less than the sample size (n), and the square root is applied to the whole quantity. In essence, this is telling you how far, on average, the individual data points differ from the mean. Thus, the greater the amount of variation among data points, the greater the standard deviation will be. Standard deviation can also be calculated using the STDEV function of Excel.

- **Confidence intervals:** A confidence interval provides a range of values that is likely to contain the "true," or *parametric*, value of the parameter (i.e., it is a range of plausible values for the parameter of interest). It is possible to test for significant differences between means by determining whether their confidence intervals overlap. The exercise at the end of Chapter 2 introduces you to the use of means and confidence intervals to test hypotheses.

A confidence interval around a particular mean is based on three quantities: the variability of the data points (standard deviation), the sample size (n), and the desired level of confidence (denoted by α, the Greek letter alpha). If we were to conduct an experiment many times and calculate a mean and confidence interval for each, then we can be confident that a proportion of these intervals equal to $1-\alpha$ should encompass the parametric mean. In most ecological studies, we require 95% confidence, and so we set the confidence level at $\alpha = 0.05$. Therefore, $1 - \alpha = 0.95$, and we are 95% confident that our observed confidence interval includes the true mean.

There are multiple ways to calculate confidence intervals, depending on the type of data and the characteristics of the data distribution. For the field studies described in this text, you can use a simple 95% CI around the mean that can be calculated using the Excel function CONFIDENCE. To do so, you will need to provide Excel with your α level (0.05), standard deviation (s), and sample size (n, the number of data points you used to calculate s). Each of these values affects the size of the confidence interval. In general, large sample sizes and small standard deviations should lead to small confidence intervals because it is easier to estimate the mean precisely if you sample many individuals and if the data are not too variable. The more stringent your confidence level, the wider the confidence interval will be; it is easier to estimate a mean with 90% certainty than it is with 95% or 99% certainty. In ecology, 95% certainty is most commonly used, as it presents a good balance.

Confidence intervals can be used for hypothesis testing. For the purposes of this course, you will use a simple, but conservative approach to testing hypotheses using confidence intervals (see Chapter 2). If the 95% CIs around two means do not overlap, reject the null hypothesis (i.e., conclude that the means are significantly different). If they do overlap, consider this to be insufficient evidence to reject the null hypothesis, and conclude that the means are not significantly different. For a more detailed treatment of the use of confidence intervals in hypothesis testing, see Cumming et al. (2007) or Julious (2004). Below, we present an example of how to test a null hypothesis using means and confidence intervals.

EXAMPLE OF CALCULATION OF CONFIDENCE INTERVALS INTERTIDAL ZONATION LAB

Table 9-1: Example data sheet for quadrat sampling

Site and Quadrat Number: Distance from High Tide Edge (meters)	Species 1: Common Periwinkle Count		Species 2: Asian Shore Crab Count		Species 3: Blue Mussel Count		Species 4: Green Crab Count	
Q1-1: Distance (m): 20	23		0		0		5	
Q1-2	11		2		0		11	
Q1-3	5		0		0		7	
Q2-1: Distance (m): 35	26							
Q2-2	28							
Q2-3	17							
Q3-1: Distance (m) 50	34							
Q3-2	25							
Q3-3	41							
Total Count at 20m	39		2		0		23	
Total Count at 35m	71							
Total Count at 50m	100							

The data in Table 9-1 are count data. Thus, we need to convert the above data to densities (organisms per square meter). If the diameter of our standard sampler is 76.2 centimeters, we divide this by 100 to get 0.762 meters. This is the diameter of our sampler in meters. To get the area of our sampler, we now use the formula for the area of a circle ($A = \pi r^2$), where the radius (r) is one half of the diameter.

Using our count data for the 20 meter sample site we get the following:

Diameter of sampler (m)	0.762
Radius of sample	0.381
π	3.14159265
Area of circular sampler (m²)	0.456
Number of samples for mean	3
Total area sampled (m²)	1.37
Total organisms counted	39
Example density (organisms/m²)	28.5

We need to do this calculation for all of the data to get the number of organisms per square meter for all the species at all three tide distances.

CALCULATION TIPS AND CONVENTIONS:

1) When you are calculating 95% confidence intervals, always calculate your mean and standard deviation using the sample data for the specific mean you are calculating. If the mean is for the density of periwinkles at 20 m for your research team, then you had 3 data values. If the mean is for the density of periwinkles on the beach (total of the 20m, 35m, and 50m sample counts) using your research team data, then you had 9 values.

2) When you calculate statistics, report means, standard deviations, and confidence intervals to one more decimal value. Use a spreadsheet, set up the sites in columns, and calculate the means and standard deviations using cell formulas at the bottom of each column. Follow the directions in the lab manual in Chapter 2 on how to use Microsoft Excel to do these calculations. These directions will also be used to plot 95% confidence intervals or error bars for each mean.

The following is an example showing how Excel can be used to convert quadrat count data for periwinkles to density data by dividing the count data by the area of the circular quadrat, which was 0.456 m^2. Thereafter, the CONFIDENCE function can be used to generate 95% confidence intervals (Table 9-2). The means and confidence intervals can be used to generate a graph that will illustrate the differences among group means (Fig. 9-2).

Table 9-2. Density of periwinkles at three locations, converted to density per m², with mean, standard deviation, and 95% CI.

Periwinkle Density				Periwinkle		Conv. to
High Tide	Mid Tide	Low Tide			Count	Density
Density	Density	Density			# per Quadrat	# per m²
41.7	46.1	59.2		Hi-Q1	19	41.7
19.7	50.4	43.9		Hi-Q2	9	19.7
8.8	30.7	72.4		Hi-Q3	4	8.8
23.4	42.4	58.5	Mean			0.0
16.8	10.4	14.3	Std._Dev.	Mid-Q1	21	46.1
19.0	11.7	16.1	95% CI	Mid-Q2	23	50.4
				Mid-Q3	14	30.7
						0.0
				Low-Q1	27	59.2
				Low-Q2	20	43.9
				Low-Q3	33	72.4

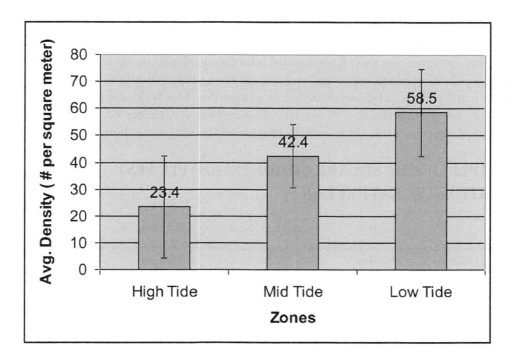

Figure 9-2. Mean and 95% CI of periwinkles at three tidal zones, from the example
data presented in Tables 9-1 and 9-2.

Based on the criteria presented above and in Chapter 2, we can use the confidence intervals
displayed in Fig. 9-2 to test for differences in mean density of periwinkles between the three
locations. Because the 95% CIs overlap for all three distances, we would fail to reject the null
hypothesis and conclude that density of periwinkles does not differ significantly among
regions of the intertidal zone.

HYPOTHESIS TESTS USING TEST STATISTICS:

In addition to comparing means by using 95% CIs, you will use two other statistical hypothesis tests in this course: chi-square goodness-of-fit tests (Chapter 6) and correlation analyses
(Chapter 8). These two types of tests address very different questions, so we will describe each
in some detail.

Chi-square goodness-of-fit test: To test hypotheses about how discrete data (i.e., counts of
individuals) are distributed among groups or categories (as introduced in Chapter 2), use a chi-
square goodness-of-fit test. Recall that the chi-square test statistic is calculated as:

$$\chi^2 = \sum_{i=1}^{k} \frac{(Observed - Expected)^2}{Expected}$$

To calculate this, therefore, you must have an expected count for each of your k categories. These expected values can come from multiple sources, including theoretical predictions (e.g., Mendelian genetics, as described in Chapter 2) and the results of previous studies. Sometimes, however, you don't have detailed information about the study system. In this case, you can use the simplest possible approach to generating expected values: assume that an individual is equally likely to belong to any of the categories. This is the approach you will use for your study on the distribution of intertidal invertebrates (Chapter 6). An example, using hypothetical data from this study, will illustrate how the analysis is done.

EXAMPLE OF CHI-SQUARE GOODNESS-OF-FIT TEST
INTERTIDAL ZONATION LAB

Table 9-3: Example data sheet for quadrat sampling.

Site and Quadrat Number: Distance from High Tide Edge (meters)	Species 1: Common Periwinkle Count		Species 2: Asian Shore Crab Count		Species 3: Blue Mussel Count		Species 4: Green Crab Count	
Q1-1: Distance (m): 20	23		0		0		5	
Q1-2	11		2		0		11	
Q1-3	5		0		0		7	
Q2-1: Distance (m): 35	26							
Q2-2	28							
Q2-3	17							
Q3-1: Distance (m) 50	34							
Q3-2	25							
Q3-3	41							
Total Count at 20 m	39		2		0		23	
Total Count at 35 m	71							
Total Count at 50 m	100							

The above data (Table 3) represent counts of four species of invertebrates at three quadrats at each of three distances from the high tide line (see Chapter 6). Suppose we want to test whether individuals are evenly distributed among the three distances. The first thing we do is to sum up the total counts of individuals at each distance. (Note, however, that for this to work we must assume that all three of our samples are estimating abundance of individuals equally accurately.) We now have *observed counts* of periwinkles at each distance (39, 71, and 100 individuals, respectively).

If we just look at those numbers, it appears that periwinkles are not evenly distributed along the intertidal zone. Instead, they seem to increase in density as distance from the high tide line increases. But is this pattern statistically significant, or could it instead have resulted simply from random variation (sampling error)? To answer this question, we first need to know the expected counts. Because we are testing the null hypothesis that there is no difference in occurrence of individuals between distances, we should expect counts to be, on average, the same for each distance. We sampled a total of 210 periwinkles (39 + 71 + 100), so our expectation would be that, if the null hypothesis is true, 1/3 of the 210 individuals should be found at each distance. Our *expected values*, therefore, are 70 at 20m, 70 at 35m, and 70 at 50m. Obviously, if our null hypothesis was different, our expected values would also be different. *In fact, sometimes the expected values will not be whole numbers. This is not a problem. Only your observed values must be discrete counts.*

Table 9-4: Observed and expected values for chi-square analysis on hypothetical periwinkle data, with intermediate steps in the calculation of the χ^2 test statistic

Periwinkles						
	Distance	Distance	Distance			
	Category	Category	Category			
	20 m	35 m	50 m			
observed	39	71	100		total	210
expected	70	70	70		average	70
$\dfrac{(\text{obs} - \text{exp})^2}{\text{exp}} =$	13.72857	0.014286	12.85714			
	$\chi^2 =$	26.6				
	Degrees of Freedom =		2			

We now compare our observed values to the expected values using the chi-square formula provided above. For our example, summarized in Table 9-4:

$$\chi^2 = \frac{(39-70)^2}{70} + \frac{(71-70)^2}{70} + \frac{(100-70)^2}{70}$$

Therefore,

$$\chi^2 = 13.72857 + 0.014286 + 12.85714 = 26.600$$

If the null hypothesis is true (i.e., your expected values are an accurate reflection of reality), then χ^2 should be close to zero, whereas if the null hypothesis is false, χ^2 should be large. But how large is large enough to give you cause to reject the null hypothesis?

Recall that the rare event rule dictates that we can reject the null hypothesis when our observed results would be unlikely to happen if the null hypothesis were true. Luckily, statisticians have determined what values of χ^2 fulfill this requirement. The "critical value" of χ^2 depends on two things: your confidence level, α (which we will set at 5%, or $\alpha = 0.05$), and the number of *degrees of freedom*, which is derived from the number of groups or categories (df = k - 1). The more stringent your confidence level and the larger the number of categories, the larger the critical value of χ^2 (Table 9-5).

Compare your calculated chi-square test statistic to the critical value for the appropriate degrees of freedom based on the number of categories in your comparison. In this example, we are comparing the total number of periwinkles at three different locations so df = $3 - 1 = 2$. The critical value of χ^2 at $\alpha = 0.05$ and 2 degrees of freedom is 5.991 (Table 9-5).

Table 9-5: Selected critical values for χ^2 if the confidence level is set at $\alpha = 0.05$ (from Rohlf and Sokal 1995).

Number of Categories (k)	Degrees of Freedom (k-1)	Critical Value of $\chi^2_{(0.05,\ k-1)}$
2	1	3.841
3	2	5.991
4	3	7.815
5	4	9.488

Show this in your report as:
$$\chi^2_{(0.05,\ 2)} = 5.991$$

Because your calculated chi-square value of 26.600 is greater than the critical value, you would **reject** your null hypothesis of no difference in the frequency of occurrence of this species between the three distances. If the calculated value was less than the critical value of Chi-square $_{(0.05,\ 2)} = 5.991$, then you would fail to reject your null hypothesis of no difference and assume the observed difference in numbers is purely due to chance variation (sampling error). Obviously, the greater the difference is between the Observed and the Expected values, the more likely you are to reject your null hypothesis.

Chi-square tests in Excel: Excel has multiple functions that are useful for conducting chi-square goodness-of-fit tests (see the exercise at the end of Chapter 2).

CHIINV: Given your α level and degrees of freedom, this function will return the critical value of χ^2. You can use this function or Table 9-5 to obtain the critical value.

CHIDIST: Given your calculated chi-square test statistic and degrees of freedom, this function will return a p-value, the probability that you would expect a value of χ^2 as extreme as you observed, if the null hypothesis were true. If this value is less than your α level (usually 0.05), this indicates that your χ^2 value is higher than the critical value, and you can reject the null hypothesis.

CHITEST: Given your observed and expected values, this function will return a p-value. If all calculations are done correctly, CHITEST and CHIDIST should generate identical p-values. Thus, you can check your work by using both.

A final word of caution about chi-square tests: Remember that analysis of count data using chi-square requires that no expected value is equal to zero and no more than 20% of the <u>expected values</u> are less than five. If your analysis does not meet these requirements, the results will be unreliable (you will be more likely to reject the null hypothesis, even if it is true). If you encounter this problem, you can either gather more data or use an alternative statistical technique.

Correlation: Often, ecologists look for relationships between variables. For example, we might want to know whether there is an association between light intensity and the growth rate of a particular plant, or whether there is an association between temperature and activity of an animal species. Or, as you will investigate in Chapter 8, we might be interested in whether the size of a tree has any relationship to the size (or the distance to) its nearest neighbor. To test for an association between two quantifiable variables, we can use a *correlation coefficient.*

There are multiple types of correlation coefficients, which differ slightly in how they are calculated. The most commonly used, and the one that you will use in this course, is Pearson's product-moment correlation coefficient, which is symbolized as r. It tells you two things: the strength of the linear relationship between two variables and whether that relationship is positive or negative. The value of r will always be between -1 and 1, inclusive. Values close to 0 indicate no relationship between the two variables, whereas values far from 0 indicate a strong relationship (see Fig. 9-3). An r of 1 indicates a perfect positive linear relationship between the variables (i.e., as x increases, y increases), and an r of -1 indicates a perfect negative linear relationship (i.e., as x increases, y decreases).

The formula to calculate r is long and complex, but you will not be expected to calculate it by hand. Instead, Excel can generate correlation coefficients for you. Simply use the function CORREL and select the appropriate columns of data, and the program will return the value of r.

Here you will encounter the same problem as you did when you calculated χ^2: how large does r have to be for you to consider the relationship between variables to be significant? As with many statistics, this decision (what is the critical value) depends on your sample size. The fewer samples you have, the higher your r must be to achieve significance, because at low sample sizes, one or two unusual individuals can dramatically influence the overall pattern you observe. For example, at $\alpha = 0.05$, the critical value for r is:
  0.632 if $n = 10$
  0.444 if $n = 20$
  0.361 if $n = 30$
  0.196 if $n = 100$ (Triola and Triola 2006).

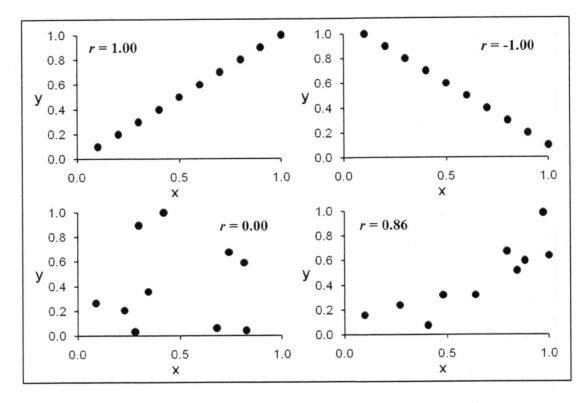

Figure 9-3. Four scatterplots that illustrate differences in correlation coefficients.

You can reject the null hypothesis that there is no association between the two variables if the **absolute value** of your calculated r is greater than or equal to the critical value.

Even if a correlation is statistically significant (i.e., not likely to have been caused by sampling error), that does not mean that the relationship is very strong. For example, an r of only 0.159 would be statistically significant if you took 150 samples, yet that is far from a perfect correlation ($r = 1.0$). You might ask, then, how strong a correlation must be before it is considered "strong." That is a point of interpretation that differs among disciplines. Many physicists and engineers, for example, require extreme precision, and only consider a correlation strong if it is well above 0.9. In ecology, on the other hand, we work with living organisms, which are highly variable in their behavior and characteristics. Therefore, we can be less restrictive. In this class, we will consider a correlation strong if $r > 0.7$ or $r < -0.7$. A significant correlation for which r does not exceed 0.5 (or -0.5) can be considered weak.

Two notes of caution regarding correlation analyses:
1. Pearson's correlation coefficient is a good general test for associations between variables, but it does have one limitation: it assumes that any relationship between the variables is at least approximately linear (see the examples in Fig. 9-3). This assumption might not always be valid. For example, consider the effect of water on growth of plants. As you add water, the plants should grow more rapidly, until you saturate the soil. Thereafter, additional water has no positive effect on growth, and may in fact harm the plants. Too much water (flooding) can kill the plants, thereby reducing growth to zero. The relationship between water and plant growth, then, is probably

non-linear; a scatterplot would show a curved response of one variable to the other. An analysis using r would not capture this relationship.

2. Be careful when interpreting correlations. In particular, keep in mind that when two variables are strongly correlated, that does not necessarily mean that one of them causes the other. There could be a causal relationship, or both variables might be responding to a third factor. For example, the number of violent crimes committed in a city per year might be strongly correlated with the number of fast food restaurants in the city, but that does not mean that fast food causes crime. Instead, both variables are probably driven by a third variable: population size.

LITERATURE CITED

Cumming, G., Fidler, F., and Vaux, D. L. 2007. Error bars in experimental biology. *Journal of Cell Biology* 177:7-11.

Julious, S. A. 2004. Using confidence intervals around individual means to assess statistical significance between two means. *Pharmaceutical Statistics* 3:217-222.

Rohlf, F. J., and Sokal, R. R. 1995. *Statistical Tables*. Third Edition. New York: W.H. Freeman and Company. 199 pp.

Triola, M. M., and Triola, M. F. 2006. *Biostatistics for the Biological and Health Sciences*. Boston: Pearson/Addison-Wesley, 699 pp.